BEYOND THE ORDINARY MIND

Beyond the Ordinary Mind

Dzogchen, Rimé, and the Path of
Perfect Wisdom

SELECTED WORKS BY
Khenpo Pema Vajra, Patrul Rinpoche,
Jamgön Mipham, Jigme Tenpe Nyima,
Amdo Geshe Jampal Rolwe Lodrö,
Yukhok Chatralwa Chöying Rangdrol,
and Dongak Chökyi Gyatso

TRANSLATED AND INTRODUCED BY
Adam Pearcey

FOREWORD BY
Alak Zenkar Rinpoche

SNOW LION
BOULDER
2018

Snow Lion
An imprint of Shambhala Publications, Inc.
2129 13th Street
Boulder, Colorado 80302
www.shambhala.com

9 8 7 6 5 4 3 2

Printed in the United States of America

Shambhala Publications makes every effort to print on acid-free, recycled paper.

Snow Lion is distributed worldwide by
Penguin Random House, Inc., and its subsidiaries.

LIBRARY OF CONGRESS CATALOGING-IN-PUBLICATION DATA
Names: O-rgyan-'jigs-med-chos-kyi-dbang-po, Dpal-sprul, 1808–1887. |
Mi-pham-rgya-mtsho, 'Jam-mgon 'Ju, 1846–1912. | Pearcey, Adam, translator.
Title: Beyond the ordinary mind: Dzogchen, Rimé, and the Path of Perfect Wisdom:
selected works / by Patrul Rinpoche, Jamgön Mipham, and other masters; translated
and introduced by Adam Pearcey.
Description: First edition. | Boulder: Snow Lion, 2018. | Includes bibliographical
references and index. | Includes translations from Tibetan.
Identifiers: LCCN 2017019422 | ISBN 9781559394703 (pbk.: alk. paper)
Subjects: LCSH: Rdzogs-chen.
Classification: LCC BQ7662.4 .B48 2018 | DDC 294.3/444—dc23
LC record available at https://lccn.loc.gov/2017019422

The pure awareness beyond the ordinary mind
Is the special feature of the Great Perfection.

–Jigme Lingpa

Contents

FOREWORD

Not so long ago I saw this anthology of writings compiled by the noted translator Adam Pearcey for his book *Beyond the Ordinary Mind*. As I read through it, I found it contained many authentic original texts, composed by authors who not only were all universally acknowledged as learned and realized masters, but who also did an enormous amount to enhance and enrich the teachings of both the New and the Ancient traditions of Tibetan Buddhism. Dzogchen Khenpo Pema Vajra, Dza Patrul Jigme Chökyi Wangpo, Jamgön Mipham Namgyal Gyatso, the Third Dodrupchen Jigme Tenpe Nyima, and Yukhok Chatralwa Chöying Rangdrol were all holders of the lineage of the Great Perfection tradition of Secret Mantra, and yet they also recognized its ultimate compatibility and harmony with other traditions. At the same time, Amdo Geshe (also widely known as Drakkar Geshe) Jampal Rolwe Lodrö, and Tulku Sungrab Dongak Chökyi Gyatso, who were both great *geshes* within the Geluk "Yellow Hat" tradition, equally established the ultimate convergence of New and Ancient Schools.

Using scriptural citation, logical reasoning, and pith instructions, these masters showed how their own traditions transcended sectarian prejudice. Likewise, they undermined false views, overcame opponents, realized all teachings to be without contradiction, and clearly perceived all the scriptures as actual, practical advice. They cared for their fortunate followers through instructions on how to integrate every aspect of the Dharma, and they ensured the continuity of the teachings through their writings. That this anthology contains so many texts by such masters makes it, to my mind, seem like an exquisite vase filled with a great treasure of wondrous and marvelous explanations.

Reading through these texts, which convey secret, crucial points of instruction on the Profound View—from the Great Perfection, the Great Seal (Mahāmudrā), and the Great Middle Way—they feel like an elixir for the eyes. Consider, for example, how these writings demonstrate so clearly the critical importance of the three essential qualifications in the Dzogchen tradition. For pure awareness—or *rigpa*—to be introduced, an authentic teacher must possess the qualities of knowing wisdom, caring love, and spiritual power. The authentic student must have faith and pure *samaya* commitments, be free from the stain of wrong view, and uncorrupted by doubt. In addition, the student's mind must be trained through authentic instructions, such as the uncommon preliminary of "destroying the house of the ordinary mind," thereby uncovering mental flaws through contemplations such as the investigation of mind's coming, staying, and going.

These various texts refer to the Great Middle Way beyond the conceptual elaborations of refutation and proof, which is a theme Mipham Rinpoche emphasizes in his sūtra-level instructions on the view of the Middle Way. This, in turn, corresponds to the Great Seal (Mahāmudrā) of the Path of Liberation in the instructions on the view bringing together sūtra and mantra from the Kagyü tradition, and to the view of the Inseparability of Saṃsāra and Nirvāṇa among the Sakya, and so on. Works that cite such themes bring together points from hundreds of sūtras, all summarized in a single instruction. I therefore am left with the impression that this collection is just like a treasury of precious jewels, or a powerful wish-granting tree capable of fulfilling every need. There is really nothing more to say than that.

Let us conclude, then, with some words from the Fourth Paṇchen Lama, Lobzang Chökyi Gyaltsen:

> Pacification (Zhijé), Severance (Chöd), the Great
> Perfection,
> Instructions on the View of the Middle Way, and the like,
> Are known by many different names,

But when an experienced yogi, who is learned in scripture
    and reasoning,
Investigates their definitive meaning, they are found to be
    of a single intention.

And from the Precious Guru Padmasambhava:

Some call it the Middle Way,
Some call it the Transcendent Perfection of Wisdom,
Some call it Essence of the sugatas,
Some call it the Great Seal,
Some call it Single All-Encompassing Sphere,
Some call it Space of Phenomenal Reality (*dharmadhātu*),
Some call it All-Ground (*ālaya*),
Some call it Ordinary Awareness—
It may be pointed out directly as follows:
Once a past thought has dissolved without trace,
In the freshness of mind before a future thought rises.
While remaining naturally without fabrication in the
    present,
If that ordinary state of consciousness
Should turn and look directly into itself,
There is clarity, in which nothing is seen through looking,
A direct form of awareness, naked and alert.
Unmade in any way, it is open and clear.
Its clarity and emptiness indivisible, it is lucid and awake.
It is not everlasting, for it is entirely uncreated.
Nor is it a void, for it is penetrating clarity.
It is not one, because it is aware of and cognizes the
    manifold.
Nor is it multiple, for it embraces all in indivisible
    experience.
And it is not found elsewhere, for it is one's very own
    awareness.

In response to a request from the Buddhist scholar, the talented translator Adam Pearcey, I, the one named Thubten Nyima, wrote this in Brooklyn, New York, on April 14, 2017. May virtue and goodness abound.

Alak Zenkar Rinpoche

Preface

Many different circumstances came together to shape and bring about this book. Several of the texts translated herein featured in my PhD research, which was itself a continuation of themes first encountered while working on His Holiness the Dalai Lama's *Mind in Comfort and Ease*, published in 2007. Two (and a half) of the introductory essays have been adapted from blogposts; many of the translations first appeared on the Lotsawa House website. Yet this collection also includes much that is new, including four previously unpublished translations together with most of the introductory material.

The arrangement of texts is roughly chronological, allowing a story to unfold over several generations of teachers and students. The general introduction and the individual essays that precede each translation—or, in chapters 3 and 4, *sets* of translations—attempt to tell this story by providing some biographical and historical background to the texts themselves. But this is not a thoroughgoing history. Rather, it is a collection of essays, poems, letters, notes, and advice, that touch upon common themes: education, (non)sectarianism, and the perfect wisdom that transcends the intellect. Names reoccur throughout the book, some well known, others perhaps less so. Texts and authors have, in fact, been chosen as much for their idiosyncrasies and what these might reveal as for their reputation or renown. After all, Tibet's great literary heritage, so much of it still awaiting the attention it deserves, contains simply untold riches, and many an untold story too.

Adam Pearcey
February, 2017

INTRODUCTION

What does it mean to go beyond the ordinary mind? For practitioners of Tibet's Great Perfection (or Dzogchen) tradition, the transcendence of ordinary concepts and mental processes marks the very beginning of the path. Once mind's true nature, which is pure, open awareness (*rigpa*), has been revealed by the teacher, the path involves nothing more than getting used to this awareness, until eventually it becomes an uninterrupted experience. Dzogchen (also known as Atiyoga) thus describes itself as an awareness-centric approach, in contrast to lesser methods based on the ordinary, discursive mind (*sem*).[1] But there is still a question as to the role of the intellect (and, by extension, scholasticism) in the Dzogchen tradition. This book attempts to address this question by looking at some of the writings of various Dzogchen masters from the last two centuries. To put these texts and their concerns into context, however, some historical background is in order.

Between the mid-nineteenth and mid-twentieth centuries, Eastern Tibet witnessed many cultural and religious changes. One particularly significant development for followers of the oldest of Tibet's four main Buddhist schools, the Nyingma or Ancient Ones, was the expansion of scholasticism within monastic communities. This school had produced its share of great scholars before—including, for example, Rongzom Chökyi Zangpo (eleventh century), Longchen Rabjam (1308–1364), and Jigme Lingpa (1730–1798)—but during this period a new intellectual movement developed. Whereas these previous masters had focused primarily on esoteric subjects, especially the tantras and the Great Perfection, their lineal descendants took a keen interest in exoteric topics as well. Senior figures such as Dza Patrul Rinpoche (1808–1887) and

Khenpo Pema Vajra (c.1807–1884), for example, composed commentaries on major Mahāyāna treatises and contributed to what was effectively a revolution in monastic education.

Some historians have linked this new scholasticism to the Rimé (nonsectarian) movement spearheaded by Jamgön Kongtrul Lodrö Taye (1813–1899) and Jamyang Khyentse Wangpo (1820–1892). It is indeed true that students and allies (and incarnations) of both masters were among those working to improve monastic learning in the Nyingma, Sakya, and Kagyü schools. However, just as relevant to the burgeoning of Nyingma scholasticism was another, lesser-known group, which E. Gene Smith referred to as the Gemang movement—named after the hermitage near Dzogchen Monastery, where the scholar Gyalse Shenpen Taye (1800–1855) lived and taught. Shenpen Taye and his followers made it their mission to revitalize monastic education and strengthen monastic discipline. Dzogchen Monastery's scriptural college (*shedra*), the famed Shri Singha, which Gyalse Shenpen Taye established in 1848, eventually became a model for the entire region, producing scores of influential scholars. Yet it was only with the remarkable career of Khenpo Shenpen Chökyi Nangwa, or Shenga (1871–1927), another member of the Gemang group and unofficially Shenpen Taye's incarnation, that this brand of monastic education in Eastern Tibet decisively took hold and spread throughout the region. Shenpen Chökyi Nangwa founded several colleges himself, trained students who established more, and wrote commentaries that became the core of the new curricula.

Shenpen Chökyi Nangwa's texts were annotated editions of Indian treatises; they therefore ignored many of the controversies that had preoccupied Tibet's scholarly minds for centuries. But while Shenpen Chökyi Nangwa focused on Indian sources, other authors preferred to emphasize what they saw as the distinctive viewpoints of their own Tibetan traditions. Jamgön Mipham (1846–1912), for instance, set out a uniquely Nyingma perspective, based on the writings of earlier scholars, especially Rongzom and Longchen Rabjam. But his treatises sparked debate, both within the Nyingma school and externally, between the Nyingma and Geluk. (A famous example was the contest between Mipham and Alak Dongak Gyatso discussed in chapter 2.) In addition, when the writings of such Sakya philosophers as Gorampa Sönam Senge (1429–1489) were reprinted and distributed during this period, they too proved contentious, reigniting age-old rivalries between the Sakya and Geluk, as is made clear in Amdo Geshe's open letter, "The Messenger of Authentic Reasoning" (chapter 10).

Quite apart from such controversies, however, the expansion of scholasticism also had an impact on the kind of literature produced and read within the Nyingma school. Among the new generation of well-educated Nyingma scholars, instructions on Dzogchen—an approach renowned today for its almost Zen-like simplicity—could, in certain contexts, be expressed and explained in the sophisticated, often abstruse language of Buddhist philosophy. This is what we find, for example, in the final testament of the scholar-monk Orgyen Tendzin Norbu (1841–1900), a prominent member of the Gemang tradition. His last words (which are the subject of chapter 6) combine a so-called lion's roar proclaiming that buddhahood is to be sought nowhere but in the very nature of one's own mind with a declaration of Dzogchen's superiority expressed through Abhidharma terminology. The language used is therefore as much a testament to his prodigious learning as it is to his commitment to, and mastery of, the Great Perfection.

Extensive erudition is equally evident in the writings of the Third Dodrupchen Jigme Tenpe Nyima (1865–1926), who was a disciple of, among others, both Mipham and Orgyen Tendzin Norbu.[2] As someone well versed in logic and philosophy and renowned for his deeper realization, Jigme Tenpe Nyima was ideally positioned to warn of scholasticism's potential dangers. His *On the Ignorance of the Learned*, the subject of chapter 7, cautions against misusing the intellect to formulate trivial arguments and seek flaws in the assertions of an imagined opponent. Such preoccupations only erode positive qualities, he explains, and squander the precious opportunity that human life affords.

Jigme Tenpe Nyima's own spiritual development provides a revealing insight into the scholasticism of the period. A child prodigy who, much to Patrul Rinpoche's delight, lectured on the *Bodhicaryāvatāra* at the age of just eight, he went on to study with both Alak Dongak Gyatso and Mipham, inevitably becoming caught, to some extent, between their opposing views. At the age of thirty-five, as foretold in a message from Mipham (translated in chapter 5), Jigme Tenpe Nyima underwent something of a midlife crisis of allegiance before reaffirming his Nyingma identity. Later in life, as an acknowledged authority on Dzogchen, he was often called upon to explain abstruse or difficult points and clarify the words of Longchen Rabjam (as in chapter 8, for example) and Jigme Lingpa. And in his answers to the questions of the young Jamyang Khyentse Chökyi Lodrö (translated in chapter 9), we see this expertise communicated alongside a caring concern for his protégé's education and the continuation of the lineage.

While Jamgön Mipham was unafraid to highlight or even promote differences between the various Tibetan schools (see chapter 3), others took a more conciliatory approach. Dongak Chökyi Gyatso (1903–1957), for instance, attempted to highlight unity rather than difference, and he made it his mission to reconcile Nyingma and Geluk views. His *Memorandum on Mahāmudrā and Dzogchen Instructions* (translated in chapter 12) demonstrates an extraordinary commitment to harmonizing. In it he suggests that the Gradual Path (*lamrim*) instructions popularized in the Geluk school should be combined with the advanced meditations of Mahāmudrā and Dzogchen to create a path suitable for the average student. He also calls upon his fellow Gelukpas to accept both the validity and the necessity of Mahāmudrā and Dzogchen practices.

By the time Dongak Chökyi Gyatso was writing, however, Mipham's characteristic explanations of emptiness and Middle Way philosophy, complete with their criticisms of key Geluk ideas, were widely studied and accepted within the Nyingma tradition. So great was Mipham's influence, in fact, that it is clearly discernible even in such a practical instruction as Yukhok Chatralwa's *How to Practice the Path of the Great Perfection* (translated in chapter 11). Some readers might find the extent of philosophical content in this text a little surprising, especially given its title, but the initial audience evidently included recipients of a shedra (or at least shedra-style) education.

Whenever appropriate, Dzogchen masters also offer less theoretical, more practical forms of guidance. One notable example is Mipham's *A Lamp to Dispel Darkness* (translated in chapter 4), through which, he tells us, even an "ordinary village yogi" can reach the level of a realized master. Reading the text's quotation of Saraha, advising us to go beyond thinking and to "remain like a young child, free of thoughts," we might even begin to question the need for training in Buddhist philosophy at all. Yet none of the authors featured in this collection endorses an anti-intellectualist approach. Most Dzogchen instruction manuals do not dwell on philosophical points, but that is because they are part of a bigger literary picture: the final layer in a three-part structure consisting of tantras, commentaries, and pith instructions. The third stage is the most concentrated and refined, but, like the leaves on a tree, it derives from, and ultimately depends upon, the trunk of canonical scripture.

Some degree of intellectual knowledge is important during the initial stages of the path. Understanding is to be cultivated through listening to and reading the teachings, then reflecting deeply upon them. After this, however, meditation is essential if understanding is to develop into genuine wisdom. Yet, ultimately, from a Dzogchen perspective, even the form of insight known as *prajñā* (*sherab* in Tibetan)—precise, discerning wisdom or intelligence— must eventually be transcended, as the whole of one's experience is transformed into the purest form of primordial wisdom. Tibetans call this second type of wisdom *yeshe*, and it is simultaneously a way of knowing—fresh, pristine awareness beyond the duality of subject and object—and a way of being—open, responsive, and uncontrived.

The method whereby the lesser insight of *prajñā* is transcended so that it can give way to pure, primordial wisdom—which is itself ordinary, in the sense of natural—is explained in detail in the Dzogchen manuals. Although some instructions of this kind are translated in the following pages, putting them into practice requires the guidance (and authorization) of a qualified teacher. Moreover, the focus here is generally on the preliminaries rather than the main practices. It is through the preliminaries that we "demolish the house of the ordinary mind," cultivating insight in order to transcend it. For all but a few supremely gifted individuals, this process must begin with analysis, but meditation remains crucial, both for stabilizing the insights gained through investigation and for allowing insight to develop into wisdom.

The notion of transcending the intellect was perhaps of special interest in an environment where scholasticism had grown in popularity and importance. This, then, is the key topic at the heart of this book: the means of making evident "nondual, primordial wisdom beyond the domain of the ordinary mind"—as Mipham puts it in *Profound Instruction on the View of the Middle Way* (translated in chapter 4). Here, Mipham writes of those "with only dry, theoretical understanding," who are "worn out by all kinds of reasoning and ideas." What they need, he says, is meditation, regular and properly graduated. And so, rather than merely provoking such theorizing and speculation—in Mipham's view as useless as descriptions of water to the thirsty—or fueling controversy and division, may what follows serve as an inspiration and reminder to put the profound instructions into practice and drink from the waters of meditation, thereby discovering what lies beyond the superficial, the partial, and the ordinary.

BEYOND THE ORDINARY MIND

A YOGI'S GUIDE TO THE DHARMA

In the two decades that have passed since the publication of Tulku Thondup Rinpoche's *Masters of Meditation and Miracles*, more information has become available about the life of Khenpo Pema Vajra (or Pema Dorje). For instance, a short biography published in 2001 provides clearer dates, noting that he was born some time before 1807 and passed away in 1884. And we now know a little more too about the important role he played as a teacher to some of the nineteenth century's most illustrious figures—including Jamgön Mipham, Orgyen Tendzin Norbu, and Jigme Tenpe Nyima, whose writings feature in the coming pages. Still, much remains unknown about Pema Vajra's many years teaching at Shri Singha college and about his activity in the hermitage in nearby Peme Tang, where he continued to grant empowerments and instructions until the end of his life.[1]

A prolific author, Khenpo Pema Vajra is said to have composed six volumes of writing, and although only a fraction of this is currently available, it is enough to reveal a broad range of interests.[2] Together with his guides to the ritual and meditation practices of the Longchen Nyingtik are notes on the *Guhyagarbha Tantra* and related topics, as well as more scholarly works, such as a short commentary on *The Ornament of Realization* (*Abhisamayālaṃkāra*), a survey of the five logical arguments of Middle Way philosophy, and an essay on *bodhicitta*. There are also texts of personal advice, letters (including one to Patrul Rinpoche), answers to students' questions, and a response to critics of the Nyingma school.

Like Patrul Rinpoche, his close contemporary and colleague at Dzogchen Monastery, Khenpo Pema Vajra grounds his scholarly writing in practical concerns. Consider, as an example, his commentary to *The Ornament of Realization*, which he wrote in 1875 to mark the enthronement of the Fifth Dzogchen Rinpoche, Tupten Chökyi Dorje (1872–1935). Of the eight topics covered in the root text, Pema Vajra's commentary dwells at greatest length on the first, omniscience, which he tells us is the most important focus not only for study and reflection but also for meditation. This puts his text in the same category as Patrul Rinpoche's commentary on *The Ornament of Realization*, entitled *Fine Explanations from the Scriptural Tradition* (or, for that matter, Patrul's *Brightly Shining Sun* on the *Bodhicaryāvatāra*)—namely, commentary as a guide for meditation.

This same concern is also in evidence in the brief overview of the Buddhist teachings translated below. While providing an accessible introduction to the three turnings of the wheel of Dharma and the Mantra collection, the text is much more than simply a taxonomy of categories and subcategories. "How do we put this into practice?" the author asks after outlining the Four Noble Truths, before relating these truths to the preliminary and main practices. As he states in the concluding verses, the author saw his text as rising above intellectual interest and speculation, just as the sun climbs over the eastern mountains. While showing the continued relevance of the Four Noble Truths throughout every level of teaching and the path, Pema Vajra's text thus blends points of instruction with points of information. The result is not dry, theoretical exposition but meditation advice within a classical framework: what we might call scholarship for yogis.

Overview of the Three Turnings and the Mantra Collection of the Vidyādharas

KHENPO PEMA VAJRA

Homage to the Buddha!

Our Teacher turned the wheel of Dharma in three stages: (1) the first turning of the wheel of Dharma on the Four Noble Truths, (2) the second turning of the wheel of Dharma on the absence of characteristics, and (3) the final turning of the wheel of Dharma on the making of perfect distinctions.

THE FIRST TURNING OF THE WHEEL OF DHARMA: THE FOUR NOBLE TRUTHS

The four truths were taught for the sake of beginners who wish to leave saṃsāra behind and attain liberation. They are explained in terms of (1) the characteristics of saṃsāra and (2) its causes, as well as (3) the characteristics of liberation and (4) the methods for attaining it.

The Buddha said:

> This is the truth of suffering.
> The truth of suffering is to be understood.
> This is the truth of the origin.
> The truth of the origin is to be abandoned.
> This is the truth of cessation.
> The truth of cessation is to be attained.

3

This is the truth of the path.
The truth of the path is to be relied upon.

1. The Truth of Suffering

The truth of suffering refers to the environments and inhabitants of saṃsāra, which can be divided further into the three realms and six classes of beings, all of which are included within the five aggregates.

How is this to be understood? There are four characteristics of suffering and saṃsāra: (1) suffering, (2) impermanence, (3) emptiness, and (4) selflessness. *Suffering* refers to the three types of suffering in saṃsāra: blatant suffering, the suffering of change, and the all-pervasive suffering of conditioning. *Impermanence* includes the coarse impermanence that is in evidence in the birth and death of beings, the formation and destruction of the universe, the changes of the seasons, and the like, as well as subtle impermanence, which is the fact that all conditioned things are constantly changing, from one moment to the next, and never remain static. *Emptiness* indicates that wherever we search, inside or outside the five aggregates, there is nothing we might call "I" or "self," just as a house is said to be empty when there is no one inside. *Selflessness* indicates that the five aggregates lack the characteristics of a self, that is, permanence, singularity, and independence. This is like saying that a house is not a person, because it lacks the characteristics of a human being.

It is necessary to understand the characteristics of the truth of suffering like this, so that we grow weary of saṃsāra and develop the wish to be liberated from it, and so that we understand how deluded it is to cling to a self where there is none.

2. The Truth of Origin

Once we have understood the truth of suffering and no longer feel any desire for it, we need to understand its cause, the reality of the origin, so that we may abandon it. For instance, when we know that physical pain is distressing and undesirable, we see the need to abandon its causes, which are sickness and harmful influences. The truth of the origin consists of two aspects: karma and mental afflictions. Karma here refers to the ten nonvirtues, tainted virtuous acts not embraced by skillful means, and mere *śamatha* (calm abiding or tranquility) that is not combined with *vipaśyanā* (clear, penetrative insight). Mental afflictions are the causes that motivate these types of action—the three main poisons of the mind together with all the primary and secondary afflictions they give rise to. The root or seed of all mental afflictions is clinging to a self. This is what we call *clinging to the self of the individual* or *innate self-clinging* and is the ignorance that is the first of the twelve links of dependent origination. Therefore, this self-clinging and all the karmic actions and afflictions that it produces are what we call origin, and we must understand how they are the causes for every kind of suffering.

Origin has four characteristics: (1) cause, (2) origin, (3) intense arising, and (4) condition. Let us explain these in the proper sequence. First, *cause* means that just as a seed produces its fruit, karma and the afflictions produce all the sufferings of saṃsāra. Second, *origin* (or source) means that just as crops grow from a field, all sufferings arise from karma and the afflictions. Third, *intense arising* means that just as when one touches a wound on the body, strong karma and afflictions immediately produce great suffering. Fourth, *condition* means that suffering is brought about through the conditions of karma and the afflictions, just as crops require conditions such as water and fertilizer for their production.

It is necessary to understand this so that we develop the wish to avoid karma, the afflictions, and self-clinging, in the same way that knowing how poison and infection are the causes of sickness leads us to strive to avoid them.

3. The Truth of Cessation

By abandoning the origin, we can be free from the sufferings of saṃsāra and realize the reality of cessation, which is nirvāṇa. We therefore need to develop the wish to realize true cessation. True cessation is unconditioned absolute space, free from the five aggregates, in which the seed of origin has been abandoned. It has four characteristics: (1) peace, (2) cessation, (3) perfection, and (4) true deliverance. *Peace* indicates that all the karma and mental afflictions, as well as suffering and the defiled conditioned phenomena that were present previously, have all been thoroughly pacified. *Cessation* means that all the seeds, which have been abandoned through applying the antidotes, will never return. *Perfection* indicates that this state is faultless, excellent, and endowed with qualities. *True deliverance* means that once we have realized cessation, it is impossible for us to return to saṃsāra ever again. Cessation, liberation, total freedom, and nirvāṇa are all synonymous.

It is necessary to understand cessation because seeing the advantages and wonderful qualities to be gained inspires us to pursue liberation.

4. The Truth of the Path

The true path is that which is practiced by an individual who knows the faults of saṃsāra's true suffering and the advantages of liberation's true cessation, and who wishes to leave saṃsāra behind and to reach nirvāṇa. The true path consists of the wisdom of not conceiving of the self of the individual, accompanied by faith, diligence, mindfulness, concentration, intelligence, and so on. It has four characteristics. It is (1) a path, (2) appropriate, (3) effective, and (4) truly delivering. It is a path since it takes us from the state of an ordinary being to awakening and liberation. It is appropriate in the sense that it is suitable as an antidote to the origin, that is, karma and the afflictions. It is effective because it unfailingly brings our minds to accomplishment on the genuine path. The path is also truly delivering because if we practice it, there is no doubt that we will be led out of, or emerge definitively from, the quagmire of saṃsāra.

How do we put this into practice? Knowing that the whole of

saṃsāra is by nature suffering, we should feel strong renunciation and a wish to escape it. We must seek a spiritual teacher who can correctly show us the path. Receiving the teacher's instructions, and guarding our pure moral discipline as carefully as our own eyes, we must accomplish stable calm and one-pointed concentration by practicing referential and nonreferential śamatha in an isolated place. Then, we must train our minds in the points of selflessness and emptiness, having discovered vipaśyanā through our teacher's instructions. Out of the unity of śamatha and vipaśyanā, we can then definitively ascertain the nature of mind itself and arouse nonconceptual wisdom in our minds. Thus, in a state of meditative equipoise unstained by attachment to experience or intellectual speculation, self-clinging will be severed at its root; fixation upon the view or meditation will fade, subtle and grosser thought states will be purified, and we will arrive at the clear, pristine natural state of consciousness that is self-knowing, devoid of any object. Until we reach this state, however, we must apply ourselves to the practice with great diligence. Once we do reach this level, quite naturally and effortlessly, we will be able to sustain its continuity through an innate mindfulness that is impervious to distraction, and through strengthening our practice, the natural radiance of unborn awareness and emptiness will become the display of uninterrupted samādhi. All types of enlightened activity for our own and others' welfare—love and compassion, faith and pure perception, generation phase (*kyerim*) and perfection phase (*dzogrim*) practice, mantra recitation, accumulation of merit and wisdom, purification of obscurations, the six perfections and four means of attraction, dedication of merit, and aspiration—will be effortlessly accomplished. Then, just as a magician conjures up magical creations or displays illusions of the four elements in the sky, all this variety will arise unceasingly as the radiance of the unborn nature and be liberated without any clinging to its display. This is how to practice enlightened action in which the two truths are inseparably united and, without any clinging or attachment, "Act, like a lotus in water, unsullied, and like the sun and moon in the sky, unhindered."³—in other words, to act without attachment or hindrance.

Let us relate this to the instructions on the preliminary practices:

- The teachings on death and impermanence and the sufferings of saṃsāra are instructions for understanding the truth of suffering.
- The teaching on the cause and effect of actions is the instruction on abandoning the true origin of suffering.
- The teaching on the benefits of liberation is the instruction on attaining true cessation.
- The teachings on contemplating the physical support with its freedoms and advantages and how to rely upon a spiritual teacher are instructions on creating the right conditions for embarking on the true path. Thereafter, the stages of the teachings from taking refuge up to guru yoga, which guide us through the three outer, inner, and secret vehicles, are the instructions for following the true path.

Therefore, since these four truths reveal the way we should practice adopting and abandoning, based on an understanding of the nature of saṃsāra and nirvāṇa, they provide a general structure for all paths and a common ground for all vehicles. They thus form the great pathway that is followed by all noble beings. This means that whatever we are practicing, whether it is the sūtras, tantras, or pith instructions, it is crucially important that we understand these truths.

THE SECOND TURNING OF THE WHEEL OF DHARMA

In the intermediate set of teachings, all phenomena are explained in terms of the three gateways to liberation: emptiness, absence of characteristics, and wishlessness. The Buddha turned the wheel of Dharma on the absence of characteristics for the benefit of disciples with the potential to follow the Mahāyāna. Self-clinging or the view of self, which is mentioned in the context of the truth of the origin as the root of saṃsāric existence, is here divided in two: clinging to the self of the individual, and clinging to a "self" or identity in phenomena. It is the clinging to a self in phenomena that is taught to be the root of saṃsāric existence. To teach its antidote, the selflessness of phenomena, in a complete way, in the context of the true path, the profound theme of emptiness is set out in extremely elaborate detail. By taking this to heart through practice, we can overcome all our cognitive obscurations and thereby realize omniscient wisdom and work for the benefit of beings for as long as space exists. Since we need to train in the boundless activity of the bodhisattvas once we have meditated on emptiness endowed with the supreme of all aspects, all the aspects of the practice of skillful means, such as arousing the supreme mind of bodhicitta, accomplishing infinite gateways to samādhi meditation, the six perfections, four immeasurables, and four means of attraction, are also taught in vast detail. In this way, we are taught to practice without dissociating skillful means from wisdom.

THE THIRD TURNING OF THE WHEEL OF DHARMA

In the final series of teachings, all phenomena are perfectly divided into three categories: imputed, dependent, and truly established. The truly established, which is the absolute truth, is taught by proving definitively that the unconditioned absolute space of all phenomena, our own naturally arising wisdom free from all conceptual elaboration, is the nature of the Great Middle Way. Any concepts of real things being existent and unreal things being empty, and even extremely subtle mental extremes, are shown to be mere conceptual ideas and subtle thought. Then, we are taught how to enter the sphere of the enlightened mind, the inconceivable wisdom in which all bases for further views have been abandoned. This too is therefore a teaching on the ultimately profound truth of the path, as a means to overcome subtle negative tendencies related to origination.

As this demonstrates, the teachings of all three turnings fall within the scope of the four truths: they do not extend beyond them but are simply subtopics within their broader framework.

THE SECRET MANTRAYĀNA

Even in the tradition of unsurpassed Secret Mantra Vajrayāna, we must realize omniscience by turning away from the causes and effects of saṃsāra and pursuing instead the causes and effects of nirvāṇa. Broadly, then, this too fits within the scheme of the four truths. Still, there is a difference in how it is put into practice.

Here we describe the environments and inhabitants of saṃsāra, which make up the truth of suffering, according to (1) how they are and (2) how they appear.

Let us first consider how things are. Underlying all these various appearances is naturally arising wisdom beyond all conceptual elaboration, the great dharmakāya in which the realities of appearance and emptiness are inseparable. We therefore speak of *the buddhahood of the spontaneously perfect ground*. As in the analogy of a jewel caked in mud, our own nature is utterly pure. The nature of the reality of suffering is true cessation, and so we speak of the indivisibility of saṃsāra and nirvāṇa. This is the continuum of the ground, or the basis for purification. To realize this, we have the view or philosophy known as *the indivisibility of saṃsāra and nirvāṇa*.

Now let us consider how things appear. Outer and inner phenomena, which appear independent in the common perception of ordinary beings, are called *deluded appearances based on a lack of realization*. This is what we must purify. It is the truth of suffering.

For the karma and mental afflictions of the truth of the origin, there are two alternatives: one is to bring them onto the path through recognizing their nature, and the other is to let them run their course and originate suffering. The way to bring them onto the path is as follows. Whichever afflictive emotion arises, if we allow ourselves to settle gently into the emotion itself, without trying to suppress or cultivate it, its energy will be released in the fundamental ground of mind, just as a block of ice melts into water or a wave dissolves into the ocean. The essence of the afflictive emotion itself, which is fundamental wisdom beyond concepts, will arise nakedly and distinctly. As this happens, there is no need to apply some other antidote: the mental affliction itself dawns as wisdom, so that the origin becomes the truth of the path. This is therefore known as *taking afflictions as the path*.

By themselves, the actions (karma) of our body and speech are neutral; it is the mind that makes them virtuous or unvirtuous. If we do not allow our minds to reify subject and object, but instead allow whatever arises in the mind to be freed within the open reality of its own intrinsic nature, that is *wisdom*. To generate bodhicitta at the outset; to practice the main part of bringing to mind deity, mantra, and samādhi so that our ordinary perception dawns as pure perception; and finally to dedicate this to the swift completion of the two accumulations is *skillful means*. When accompanied by this special wisdom and skillful means, our actions become the true path.

As for how actions become the origin, if we do not have this special wisdom and skillful means, we slip into ordinary patterns of both intention and action and, by doing so, accumulate karma, as a result of which we are compelled to wander endlessly in saṃsāra. This is how actions become the true origin of suffering.

Therefore, if we understand the key points of Vajrayāna like this and have the confidence of realization and experience, we can recognize the nature of the reality of suffering to be cessation and take the origin as the true path, so that the causes and effects of saṃsāra become the causes and effects of nirvāṇa. What is to be abandoned becomes the remedy, and we gain the realization of the indivisibility of saṃsāra and nirvāṇa.

Understanding this, we can see that there is only a slight difference between the *pratimokṣa*, bodhisattva, and Mantrayāna vows in relation to the truth of the path: whether we practice avoidance, transformation, or turning into the path. In fact, all three approaches are identical insofar as they enable us to overcome actual karma and mental afflictions; purify our habitual perception of saṃsāra, which is the truth of suffering; and realize the ultimate reality of cessation.

It is because the approach of Secret Mantra also falls within the approach of the four truths that the "essence of dependent origination" dhāraṇī,[4] which sets out the meaning of the four truths, is universally praised as supreme and is found throughout all the sūtras, tantras, and pith instructions.

These four truths, the direct teaching of the first turning,
Whose meaning is captured in a single verse in the essence of
   interdependence,
Are here set out in an original and fine explanation
Showing how to proceed in stages along the path of all the sūtras,
   tantras, and pith instructions.

This was drawn out of the great ocean of Mañjuśrī's wisdom
By the playful intervention of the goddess Sarasvatī,
To bring delight to the minds of the fortunate,
Just as the sound of her vīṇā related it to me.

Over the peaks of the intellect's eastern mountains,
May this youthful sun of instruction shine its countless rays,
Causing the thousand-petaled lotuses of faith and wisdom to
   bloom
And emit the sweet scent of experience and realization in all
   directions!

This was written by Pema Vajra. May it be virtuous!

2

THE CONSOLATION OF SOLITUDE

What little we know about Alak Dongak Gyatso (or Japa Dongak, as he is also called)[1] has all too often been presented as footnotes in the biographies of his more illustrious contemporaries. In the story of Dza Patrul Rinpoche, for instance, he appears as a student and intermediary, attempting to arrange a meeting between Patrul and the poet and yogi Shabkar Tsokdruk Rangdrol (1781–1851). The meeting never took place, but Patrul did set out on the journey, only learning of Shabkar's death after he had already traveled as far as Golok. Then, in Jamgön Mipham's biography, Alak Dongak is cast in the role of misguided opponent, a hapless scholar who loses to Mipham in a debate:

> Japa Dongak, a great scholar of the new traditions, stated that there were some invalid arguments in Mipham's commentary on the wisdom chapter of the *Bodhicaryāvatāra*. The foremost of learned, disciplined, and accomplished masters, Patrul Rinpoche, was engaged to judge, and the debate continued for several days. Most spectators could only say which arguments were in accord with their own position; they could not tell who had won and who had lost. When Lama Rigchok asked Patrul Rinpoche which of the pair was the winner, he said, "I don't know if I can be the one to decide this or whether I can put an end to it. It is rather like the saying, 'It is not for a father to praise his son, but for his enemies. It is not for a mother to praise her daughter, but for the community.' Accordingly, Dongak's monks told me that early in the debate they clearly saw a ray

of light emanate from the heart of Lama Mipham's image of Mañjuśrī, the representation of his yidam deity, and connect with the lama's heart. That really says it all.[2]

Some accounts of the same debate mention that at its conclusion Alak Dongak was forced to burn a treatise he had written on Dzogchen. Khetsun Sangpo Rinpoche said that Alak Dongak was so upset at losing and then seeing his treatise cast into the flames that he broke down and wept.[3] Tulku Thondup Rinpoche also heard the same story of Alak Dongak's distress, but he offers another possible explanation:

> Khenpo Chemchok, my own teacher, used to say that Könme Khenpo, my predecessor, once asked Alak Dongak if it was true that he cried after the debate with Mipham. He replied that he had wept, but not because he lost the argument. It was because Patrul Rinpoche chastised him. Whenever he was winning, Patrul would say, "I told you to meditate on love and compassion, but instead you have filled your head with all this intellectualizing!" Yet whenever it was Mipham who appeared to be ahead, Patrul Rinpoche offered no such criticism. Alak Dongak told Patrul, "I did not neglect your instructions. I have meditated on bodhicitta." But it was the accusation of failing to apply his teacher's instructions, rather than the humiliation of losing, that made him weep.[4]

Whatever the reasons might have been, for Alak Dongak to be represented in a state of sadness like this is rare in Tibetan Buddhist literature. It illustrates what Janet Gyatso has called a "complicated dialectic" between appreciating the greatness of adepts on the one hand, and seeing them as imperfect or complicated human beings on the other.[5] Whether we should regard Alak Dongak as imperfect is of course debatable (no pun intended), but any such judgment is hindered by a lack of biographical material and the fact that his own writings have not survived.

In the absence of any texts, it is difficult to say what it was that Alak Dongak objected to in Mipham's commentary on the wisdom chapter of the *Bodhicaryāvatāra*. Yet we do know at least some of what it was that Mipham objected to in Alak Dongak's views on Dzogchen. That is because Mipham names his opponent in his most important Dzogchen work, *Trilogy on Fundamental Mind*—a set of texts, it should be noted, that was completed and published only after Mipham's death. Essentially, Mipham rejects Alak Dongak's identification of the pure awareness of Dzogchen with the "fundamental mind" described in the *Guhyasamāja Tantra*, because he claims that both are subtle forms of ordinary consciousness. This is not permissible, says Mipham, because it would imply that rigpa arises from causes and conditions, whereas in fact rigpa, unlike the ordinary mind, is beyond causality; it is unborn and therefore unceasing.

The only sources of information about Alak Dongak himself are the brief references already given, in addition to one or two recent biographical sketches—except, that is, for a series of verses offering advice on retreat, which Patrul Rinpoche wrote for Alak Dongak and are translated below. As one recent biography claims that Alak Dongak went into retreat shortly after the debate, it is tempting to see references to the contest within these verses. When, for example, Patrul says that his words are "to dispel the sadness of a dear friend," could this be the sadness that Alak Dongak felt after losing the debate? Unfortunately, there is not enough information in the text to be sure.

Given Patrul Rinpoche's reported comments to Alak Dongak during the debate, it is interesting to note how critical he is of scholasticism in his advice. He speaks, for example, of the "hollow, husk-like words of scholars" and stresses that there is "no need for the many tools of varied fields of knowledge." By the same token, he emphasizes the importance of cultivating renunciation, love, and compassion above all else. And references to the higher teachings, such as Dzogchen, are conspicuous by their absence. As so often in his writings, Patrul Rinpoche is self-deprecating, referring to himself as an "old dog," "wicked," and "ragged Abu." There is a poignancy to his encouragements to Alak Dongak to remain in solitude for nine years, even if it means they will never meet again. Indeed, if the text was written after the debate, Patrul Rinpoche would not live much longer.

What follows, then, is more than just a poem of advice on the importance of remaining in solitude. It offers Patrul Rinpoche's views on a subject close to his own heart: he spent most of his life in retreat and even wrote this text while residing in "the mountain solitude of Dhichung." But it is also one of the few surviving textual clues to the mysterious life of Alak Dongak. And if we read it as a moving attempt to console a dear but despondent disciple, then it has a further dimension, as an encouragement to respond to an ordinary human situation by transcending ordinary human limitations.

Uniting Outer and Inner Solitude:
Advice for Alak Dongak Gyatso

PATRUL RINPOCHE

Before the holy nyagrodha, the very best of trees,
All alone, you tamed Māra and his many armies
Simply through the force of your loving-kindness—
Supreme guide who attained full awakening, care for me!

O Protector, you renounced the kingdom of a universal monarch,
Casting it aside as if it were nothing more than poisoned food.
And, all alone, you departed for the quiet of the forest,
There to accomplish single-pointed meditation—thus we have
   heard.

Therefore, these delightful mountain solitudes
Are like the family estate to the supreme guide's heirs,
And, as the best of protectors himself has said,
To rely on solitude is indeed the pinnacle of joys!

Forests, hermitages, and isolated dwelling places—
These are the outer solitude of the Victor's heirs.
Avoiding selfishness and fainthearted fears—
This is the bodhisattvas' internal isolation.

Keeping, therefore, to outer forms of solitude,
Tame the inner afflictions through tranquillity and insight
And aspire to the supreme conduct of Samantabhadra—
Possessing such good fortune one is truly the Buddha's heir.

With sweetly cascading mountain streams,
Rocky mountain shelters ascending to heaven,
And gently falling dewdrops of whitest moonlight,
This mountain retreat surpasses even the deva realm.

The dance of the slender trees does not stir the passions,
And sweet birdsong brings neither attachment nor aversion,
Enveloped in nonconceptuality's gentle, cooling shade—
Such youthful companionship is surely better than a silent void!

Undisturbed by noisy chatter, that thorn in meditation's side,
Alone in this excellent place of unattended solitude,
The old monkey of the mind has nowhere left to roam
And, settling down within, finds satisfaction.

Under the bright, oppressive sunlight of busy, bustling crowds,
Our faults and unhelpful thoughts eclipse the constellations,
But when embraced by threefold solitude's cooling nectar beams,
Such faults can easily be overcome through proper antidotes.

When it is undisturbed by rippling thoughts of sadness,
The pool-like surface of the mind is still, unmoving,
And faith and compassion's reflections readily arise.
In such constancy, what need is there for a companion?

If the mirror of mind is wiped clean, time and again,
And uncluttered with objects or circumstances,
Study, reflection, and meditation present a clear impression.
What is there to prevent the dawn of Dharma's light?

Hunger, thirst, cold, and the like—all forms of physical
    affliction—
Together with sadness, fear, and all such mental suffering,
Can, through the teachings, enhance the purifying path
And, unburdened by avoidance or indulgence, adorn the mind!

The pleasures of the five senses, longed for by the foolish,
Are not to be found in solitude as they are among the devas,
But joys of Dharma in their hundreds, lauded by the wise,
Are greater in a lonely forest than in Tuṣita's paradise.

To the bodhisattva who sees suffering as a spur to diligence,
There is nothing that could conflict with Dharma practice.
Should hundreds or thousands of demonic hordes arise as foes,
How could they affect the wise for whom adversities are allies?

Savor the fine fruit of the teacher's nectar-like instructions;
Do not chase the hollow, husk-like words of scholars.
Seek the bright luminescence of the bodhisattvas' compassion;
Do not hanker after the flickering lights of ordinary talk.

Like a smith skillfully taming and ornamenting the mind,
With no need for the many tools of varied fields of knowledge,
It's enough to take up the blade of renunciation and compassion,
Thereby to transform a negative character's stubborn hide.

A single nectar shower of the teacher's compassion
Can cause the ripening crop of qualities to grow,
As the clouds of devotion amass again and again,
And there's no need to fear an untimely frost.

Love and affection are all the greater
For friends, teachers, and family living far away,
But it's hard to feel so when they are close by,
As intimacy only incites irritation!

Faith and compassionate love, cultivated in solitude,
For the lofty, the lowly, and those in between,
Tied to enlightened action with the rope of aspiration,
Will never come undone throughout our future lives.

Even the vast scented leaves of empty talk and words
Can be embraced by the harsh touch of a serpent's evil,
But for one who has grasped the subtle meaning, like sandalwood,
What sadness is there in separation from an old dog like me?

If this old dog survives and is still here nine years hence,
There'll be time to hear his barking speeches once again,
But noble beings are fashioned by the warmth of experience,
And while the breath has not yet faded, it is wrong to delay.

The supreme, gracious teacher is like all the buddhas in person,
So let his ambrosial teaching seep into the center of your heart.
And if, through diligent practice, you imbibe the vital essence,
It's well known that you'll attain immortality in this very life!

Merely to remain in solitude without taming the mind
Is to be like wild woodland beasts and birds,
As the supreme Victorious One himself has said.
Vital it is, then, to unite outer and inner solitude!

Pride at the thought of having tamed the mind
After simply pacifying a single thought or emotion,
And contempt for those who are preoccupied—
These are hooks of Māra for those in retreat.

Pay no heed, therefore, to others' vices or virtues,
And inspire yourself with enthusiasm for Dharma.
For who is happier than the host of the event
At which the mind is seen to be mere illusion?

All the various thoughts are laid out like the features of a game
For the childlike power of awareness to play with nonattachment.
The old mothers of the six realms take their seats as compassion's
    focus,

And the offerings, sources of merit, are shared by dedication's
  skillful hand.

All this talk of realizing and seeing: it's all so hollow!
Forget bliss and clarity: they are just temporary highs!
Cultivate emptiness of which compassion is the essence,
And your own and others' welfare is assured, it is said.

Even a hundred years of exertion born of expectation for reward
Will only postpone the supreme accomplishment, we are told.
But on the path of the six perfections free from sevenfold
  attachment,[6]
Even without enlightenment in this lifetime, there'll be no
  regret!

First you met a supremely qualified guide,
Then you felt renunciation and joy for the Dharma,
And now you are meditating in woodland solitude.
O my fortunate friend, you are fortunate indeed!

I met noble masters but failed to follow them properly.
Whatever Dharma I practice, I don't apply it to my mind.
I took to solitude but couldn't be diligent or undistracted.
Turning into an old dog like me means remaining malign!

My friend, you have set out on the way to every happiness,
But as you tirelessly cultivate diligence and devotion,
Be ever watchful, alert for the demon of arrogant pride,
And your life will end happily too—do you understand?

Not ruining the mind with false visions of deities or demons,
But furnishing it with the treasures of jewel-like qualities,
May you follow in the footsteps of the great Kadampa saints.
This is my prayer: Original Protector, please bear witness!

Even if wicked old Abu should die and fall into the lower realms,
There'll come a time when he is freed through the teacher's
kindness.
Then, I pray, may he continue to uphold supreme enlightened
action
For as long as all beings, his very own mothers, still remain!

These sincere words, which arose like a rainbow from the mouth,
Were offered from the mountain solitude of Dhichung by ragged
Abu
To dispel the sadness of a dear, like-minded friend.
May their meaning become apparent!

3

THE RIMÉ OF THE ANCIENTS'
MONK-SCHOLAR

To researchers, the life of Jamgön Mipham represents something of a puzzle, if not an outright paradox. Although he is often described as ecumenical and was certainly a close disciple of the Rimé movement's founders, he devoted his entire life to redefining and promoting a uniquely Nyingma perspective. A degree of subtlety, or even flexibility, is therefore required when articulating Mipham's position on nonsectarianism.

Unquestionably, Mipham demonstrates in his writings an openness toward the various levels and forms of Buddhist teaching in general, one that sets him apart from other figures of comparable stature in Tibetan intellectual history. (Yet in this he was also following his own teacher, Patrul Rinpoche, who criticized the view that the traditions of Nāgārjuna and Asaṅga are incompatible, as well as exclusive reliance on either the second or third turning of the wheel of Dharma.) For Mipham, this accommodating attitude toward the Buddhist teachings did not always extend to the other Tibetan schools—at least not in quite the same way. Indeed, his very openness itself proved to be a point of contention. What is more, Mipham did not shy away from controversy and was willing to point out what he saw as flaws in other systems, even as he cautioned against outright hostility.

This delicate balance of being critical yet inoffensive is in evidence in two short texts of advice that Mipham wrote describing the four main schools of Tibetan Buddhism: Nyingma, Sakya, Kagyü, and Geluk (or Gendenpa, as Mipham prefers). In both, he warns against sectarian rivalry. "Any feelings of hostility will bring great ruin," he writes in "Wondrous Talk Brought About by

Conversing with a Friend," "so instead let us regard one another with joy." And in the shorter "The Four Dharma Traditions of the Land of Tibet," he advises, "while focusing on your own tradition, avoid belittling others." This is his central message, but he also uses "Wondrous Talk" as an excuse to poke fun at the different schools, including his own, satirizing what he takes to be their failings. His mockery is not intended to cause offense or undermine the kind of mutual respect and pure perception he also encourages. But it is not to be dismissed entirely either. To borrow his own image of the various schools as children of the same parents, his satire is like the teasing that often goes on between close family members: playful yet pointed, and therefore potentially useful as a means of communicating difficult truths.

Wondrous Talk Brought About by Conversing with a Friend

JAMGÖN MIPHAM

Namo mañjuśrīye!

Through the enlightened activity of the victorious buddhas
And the skillful means of their bodhisattva heirs,
May the four schools of Buddhist teachings, old and new,
Successfully transmit their perfect methods of awakening!

The transmission of sūtras has fallen to the Gendenpas,
The transmission of mantra has fallen to the Nyingmapas,
The transmission of exposition has fallen to the Sakyapas,
And the transmission of practice has fallen to the Kagyüpas.

The Sakyapas are masters of learning,
The Gendenpas are masters of discourse,
The Kagyüpas are masters of realization,
And the Nyingmapas are masters of spiritual power.

There are four marvelous transmissions:
The view beyond all extremes among Nyingmapas,
Perseverance in meditation among Kagyüpas,
Perfect conduct among Gendenpas,
And regular approach and accomplishment practice among
    Sakyapas.
Although for them all everything is complete,
Each school emphasizes a particular discipline.

Nyingmapas chant through their noses,
Sakyapas intone with their lips,
Gendenpas sing mainly through their throats,
And Kagyüpas chant strongly from within.

Gendenpas are like the body of the teachings, with the path of
scriptural study complete.
Sakyapas are like the eyes of the teachings, uniting the twin
elements of sūtra and mantra.
Kagyüpas are like the heart of the teachings, bringing devotion
into the practice.
And Nyingmapas are like the life force of the teachings, holding
the profound key instructions for the tantras and sādhanas.

Now for a few words in jest: Nyingmapas claim to have a path
for accomplishing the level of Vajradhara through the practice of
the clear light Great Perfection, without the need to rely upon an
external activity-mudrā (consort). And yet the lamas say they must
take a wife to increase their longevity, improve the clarity of their
vision, maintain good health, and benefit beings through the revelation of terma. They don't say that for the sake of the teachings
they should teach and practice! That taking a wife could be a way
to benefit the teachings and beings, and a substitute for teaching
and practice, and at the same time improve clarity of vision and the
like is, I think, incredible!

Gendenpas assert that the antidote to all the pains of existence
is the wisdom that realizes selflessness. And yet they say that when
approaching the realization of no-self there can be such a fear of
letting go of this sense of identity that it becomes difficult to sit still
upon the cushion. In the past, it was said that the attainment of the
path of seeing and the clear experience of selflessness that precedes
it are marked by special feelings of joy, so I wonder if this might be
a symptom of the current degenerate age!

Sakyapas accept the Highest Yoga tantras that affirm that inner
wisdom is primary, without regard to conduct. And yet when they

recite the Path Stage sādhana,[1] they maintain the discipline of never leaving their seats, for to do so would transgress their vow. It seems that if they ever need to get up and do something, they must crawl and drag their seat behind, which might bring temporary physical purification and liberation. Still, I wonder what would happen if they ever stood up!

Kagyüpas assert that the Great Seal (Mahāmudrā) is the primordial wisdom that pervades all saṃsāra and nirvāṇa, and yet they explain the word *mudrā* by referring to a hand.[2] What would such an enormous hand be like? I think it would be a marvelous sight.

Ha ha! That was all said in jest.

There is great significance to the sayings of the great masters of
     the past,
And there are key points to the intentions of each school, old and
     new.

What is more, most followers of the Nyingma school shun the taking of life but presume there is no need to give up women. If they are genuine yogins, I take refuge in them! But, in general, this ordinary sexual desire is harmful to the Nyingma teachings, so take care, I pray!

Most followers of the Kagyü school dislike classical exposition and logic, preferring to consider only the mind. If they are those in whom realization and liberation are simultaneous, I take refuge! But, in general, such closed-mindedness is harmful to the Kagyü teachings and must therefore be abandoned!

Most followers of the Genden school shun alcohol and the like, making them exemplary models of the teaching. Still, most see no faults in those who seek to kill and injure others. But such hostility is a great enemy, so take care, I pray!

Most followers of the Sakya school regard as supreme only those empowerments and instructions they themselves have received and the branch to which they belong—whether Sakya, Ngor, or another—but this strong prejudice and dogmatism is harmful to the Sakya teachings, so it must be abandoned!

Generally, even if we are attached to our own tradition, it is important that we have no antipathy toward other traditions. Considering our own tradition, given that we are all followers of the Buddha, we can have a close affection for one another. Then, concerning the different systems of teaching, they began from the time of Khenpo Śāntarakṣita, Guru Rinpoche, and King Trisong Detsen. As a legacy of that excellent past, all of us here in Tibet accept the four seals that are the hallmark of the Buddhist teachings.[3] We are all equal in this respect, and, what is more, we all assert the great emptiness, free from conceptual elaboration. Not only that, we all accept the Mantrayāna with its inseparable unity of bliss and emptiness. This means that, with our similar views and tenets, we are extremely close.

Those who practice other traditions, non-Buddhist outsiders and barbarians, who differ from us even in outer signs and dress, are as numerous as the stars in the night sky. Compared to them, we Buddhists are as rare as stars in broad daylight. Now, when the Buddhist teachings are on the verge of extinction, all who seek to ensure their survival must view one another as the closest of allies. Any feelings of hostility will bring great ruin, so instead let us regard one another with joy, like a mother seeing her only child or a beggar discovering a priceless treasure.

Having become followers of one teacher,
May all students of these same teachings
Abandon hostility and prejudiced views
And work together with a sense of joy!

Whatever falls outside the scope of the teachings,
Whether it is found in ourselves or others, we must abandon.
Whatever is in accord with the teachings,
Whether it belongs to us or others, we must cultivate.

Through the power of this, here within the Land of Snows,
May the four great lineages of practice, methods of victorious
buddhahood,
Blaze with the beauty of a wealth of Dharma teachings
And meet with complete and universal success!

*Mati, who knows the nature of all four schools—Sakya, Nyingma,
Kagyü, and Geluk—wrote this in jest for a friend. Maṅgalam!*

The Four Dharma Traditions of the Land of Tibet

JAMGÖN MIPHAM

Nyingma followers of Secret Mantra emphasize the actual tantra.[4]
They pursue the highest view and delight in conduct that is stable.
Most reach the vidyādhara levels and attain accomplishment,
And many are practitioners of mantra, whose power is greater
    than others.

Kagyü followers, the protectors of beings, emphasize devotion.
Many find that receiving the lineage's blessings is sufficient.
Through perseverance in the practice, most gain accomplishment.
They are similar to, and mix together with, the Nyingmapas.

The Riwo Gendenpas[5] emphasize the ways of the learned.
They are fond of analytical meditation and delight in debate,
And they impress all with their elegant, exemplary conduct.
They are popular and prosperous and put effort into learning.

The glorious Sakyapas emphasize approach and accomplishment.
Many are blessed through the power of recitation and
    visualization.
They value their own ways, and their regular practice is excellent.
When compared to other schools, they have something of them all.

Ema! All four Dharma traditions of this land of Tibet
Have but one real source, even if they arose individually.
Whichever one you follow, if you practice it properly,
Can bring qualities of learning and accomplishment.

So, like children of the same father and the same mother,
Cultivate mutual accord, devotion, and pure perception,
And, while focusing on your own tradition, avoid belittling
   others.
If you act in this way, you will also be of service to the teachings.

*I, Mipham, wrote this on the thirtieth day of the first month of the
Fire Monkey year (1896). Maṅgalam!*

4

ANALYSIS AND WHAT LIES BEYOND

Toward the end of the Iron Hare Year (1891), when Mipham was forty-five years old, he wrote a short text outlining a contemplation through which we can focus on someone for whom we feel attraction or attachment. Picturing this person in the mind's eye, we consider how they are in fact an assemblage of parts. They are, for example, made up of the five skandhas, or psychophysical aggregates: form, sensation, perception, formations, and consciousness. And even the first of these, the physical body, is made up of various parts, or, as Mipham puts it, "substances, varied and impure." These parts are themselves divisible, all the way down to the level of subtle particles.

Mipham encourages us to reflect like this, as if carrying out a virtual vivisection, repeatedly and in detail, and then, by applying the same principle to the other aggregates, to scrutinize feelings, perceptions, thoughts, and other mental phenomena. Eventually, we will discover through this that the object of our attachment is not at all as we had imagined. Rather than a single individual—the word, from the Latin *individuus*, means "indivisible"—the person is, in fact, a mass of parts, all of them insubstantial and impermanent. There is no lasting identity to any of the components, and so they are without a "self." What is more, all these ephemeral, selfless parts are bound up with suffering, as they are either painful in the present moment to some degree or serve as a basis for such pain in the future.

Mipham recommends reflecting on these points repeatedly. He uses the image of a wheel that is constantly in motion—and he called his text "The Wheel of Analytical Meditation."[1] The effect of such sustained analysis, he says, will be a reduction in desire and other disruptive mental states. The resulting calm upon the surface of the mind is a precondition for progressing along the path. Once this tranquillity has been achieved, the next stage is to gain confidence or certainty about the absence of inherent existence in all phenomena. And eventually, all conceptual notions will fade away completely within an experience of emptiness, or *śūnyatā*.

Just over a year after writing "The Wheel of Analytical Meditation," Mipham wrote another short text called "Profound Instruction on the View of the Middle Way." Although it concerns the same themes, the second work concentrates on the later stages of the path, especially how insight into the absence of self develops and deepens into genuine, ultimate wisdom and realization. To explain this, he refers to two kinds of ultimate truth: a provisional ultimate that can be conceptualized and a definitive ultimate that is beyond conceptualization. (This is not a distinction that Mipham himself invented but one that he repeatedly employs throughout his writings.) The conceptual ultimate is a necessary step, he stresses, but no more than that. The genuine, definitive ultimate can be known only through personal experience in meditation. This is not to say that it is an *object* known by a separate subject—that would be dualistic, whereas this is nondual wisdom beyond the ordinary mind. Although Mipham calls the meditation in which nondual wisdom is experienced "the yoga of the Great Middle Way," he also says that the swiftest method is to follow the pith instructions of the Mantra Vehicle, which would include the brief Dzogchen texts translated later in this chapter.

Profound Instruction on the
View of the Middle Way

JAMGÖN MIPHAM

Namo mañjuśrīye!

Once you have gone through the training in analysis
And developed confidence in the crucial point
Of how the individual is devoid of self,
Then consider how, just as the so-called "I" is
An unexamined conceptual imputation,
All phenomena included within
The five skandhas and the unconditioned are the same:
Labeled conceptually as this or that.

Although we apprehend all these various phenomena,
When we investigate and search for what is behind the label,
    it cannot be found.
And when we reach the ultimate two indivisibles,
Even the most subtle and infinitesimal cannot be established.
It is the same for all that appears through dependent origination:
Entities themselves arise dependently,
Whereas "nonentities" are dependently imputed.

So, whether an entity or nonentity,
Whatever is conceived of uncritically,
Once it is analyzed and investigated,
Is found to be without basis or origin—
Appearing yet unreal, like an illusion, dream,
Reflected moon, echo, city in the clouds,

Hallucination, mirage, and the like.
Appearing yet empty, empty yet appearing—
Meditate on the way empty appearances resemble illusions.

This is the ultimate that is categorized conceptually.
It has the confidence of a mind of understanding
And is indeed the stainless wisdom of seeing
The illusory nature of postmeditative experience.
Yet it is not yet free from focus on apprehended objects,
Nor have the features of a subjective mind been overcome,
And so, since it has not gone beyond conceptuality,
The true reality of natural simplicity is not seen.

Once this kind of certainty has arisen,
Even clinging to mere illusion
Can be understood as conceptual imputation.
There is apprehension, but no essential nature to the perceived,
And even the perceiving mind cannot be found,
So, without clinging, one is brought to rest in natural ease.

Remain like this, and all perceptions,
Both external and internal, are not interrupted.
Yet within this fundamental nature, free from grasping,
All projections imposed upon phenomena
Have never arisen and never ceased to be.
So, free from the duality of perceiver and perceived,
We rest in the all-pervading space of equality.
This is beyond assertions such as "is" or "is not."
And, within this inexpressible state of true and natural rest,
An experience dawns that is free from the slightest trace of doubt.

This is the actual nature of all things,
The ultimate that cannot be conceptualized
And can only be known individually—
The nonconceptual wisdom of meditative equipoise.

Once you become familiar with this state,
In which emptiness and dependent arising are an inseparable
    unity,
The ultimate condition in which the two truths cannot be
    separated,
That is the yoga of the Great Middle Way.

Those who wish to realize this swiftly
And make evident nondual, primordial wisdom
Beyond the domain of the ordinary mind
Should meditate on the pith instructions of Secret Mantra.

This is the ultimate profound and crucial point
Of the progressive meditations on the Middle Way.

So, begin by thoroughly refining your conduct,
And then arrive at certainty, experientially and in stages.
With confidence in the illusory nature of empty appearance,
This is what it means for nothing to be removed or added on the
    path.
And, within the equality of the all-pervading space of perfect
    wisdom,
There is complete liberation.

In a place where people suffer drought and dehydration,
Hearing that there is water does not dispel thirst;
It is only in drinking that relief is found.
And this is how it is for learning and experience, so the sūtras say.
Someone with only dry, theoretical understanding,
Who is worn out by all kinds of reasoning and ideas,
Does not need sporadic practice but, when meditating in proper
    stages,
Will swiftly gain acceptance of the profound.

Jampal Gyepe Dorje wrote down whatever came to mind on the twenty-ninth day of the eleventh month of the Water Dragon year (1892). Through this, may all beings realize the meaning of the profound Middle Way! Maṅgalam!

The Essence of Mind

Jamgön Mipham

Namo guru mañjuśrīye!

The actual nature of things is inconceivable and inexpressible. Yet, for those fortunate individuals who seek to penetrate the profound meaning of *dharmatā*, I shall offer here a few words by way of illustration.

What we call the essence of mind is the actual face of unconditioned pure awareness, recognized through receiving the guru's blessings and instructions. If you wonder what this is like, it is empty in its essence, beyond conceptual reference; it is cognizant by nature, spontaneously present; and it is all-pervasive and unobstructed in its compassionate energy. This is the pure awareness (rigpa) in which the three kāyas are inseparable. It is just as the vidyādhara Garab Dorje says in his *Final Testament*:

> This awareness, which has no concrete existence as anything at all,
> Is completely unobstructed in the arising of what are its aspects.

To summarize, the actual nature of mind—the way it has always been, in and of itself—is innate pure awareness, unfabricated and unrestricted. When this is explained in negative terms, it is not something to be apprehended, nor is it a nonexistent void. Nor is it some combination of these two or some third option that is neither. This is the view of the absence of any identifiable existence, the fact that it cannot be conceptualized in any way with the thought "It is like this." When explained in more positive, experiential terms, it is said to be manifestly empty, lucidly clear, vividly pure, perfectly even, expansively open, and so on. This can be illustrated using similes. Without limit or center, it is like space. In its limitless clarity, it is like sunlight flooding the sky. Transparent inside and out, it is like a crystal ball. In its freedom from clinging and attachment, it is like the traceless path of a bird in flight. And, beyond arising and ceasing, it is like the sky.

To dispel any doubts or misunderstandings that might arise from this instruction, it is described as the great clarity that is beyond partiality, the great emptiness of freedom from conceptual reference, the great union that cannot be separated, and so on.

The meaning here cannot be pointed out in words, for it is inexpressible; it cannot be known with ordinary modes of consciousness and is therefore inconceivable; and as it is does not fall into any extreme, it is the great freedom from elaboration. In the end, it is beyond all expressions, such as, it is all and everything; it is not all; everything lies within it; or does not, and so on. It must therefore remain an individual experience, to be realized through self-knowing awareness. The names used to illustrate this are *primordial purity* and *spontaneous presence*. But it can be summed up as the single, all-encompassing sphere of naturally arising wisdom. As it is the pinnacle of all in terms of the qualities it possesses, it is also the transcendent perfection of wisdom (*prajñāpāramitā*) and so on. It is pointed out symbolically by the sun or a magnifying glass, a crystal ball, or a finger pointing into space, and so forth.

When you have such a precious jewel in your own hand,
Even if others should discard theirs, why be angry?
Without losing your connection to these instructions,
The pinnacle of Dharma, and your own good fortune,
Even if others should criticize them, why be angry?

The Essence of Wisdom:
How to Sustain the Face of Rigpa

JAMGÖN MIPHAM

To the glorious primordial protector, I pay homage!

There are three stages to sustaining the essence of rigpa: (1) recognition, (2) perfecting the strength, and (3) gaining stability.

At first, refine your understanding until, through the guru's instructions, you come to see the actual face of rigpa, nakedly and without intellectual speculation. Once you arrive at certainty, it is crucially important that you sustain rigpa's essence by yourself. Mere recognition is insufficient; you must develop its strength. Moreover, although you might recognize rigpa at first, unless you settle in that recognition, it will soon be interrupted by thoughts, making it difficult to experience naked, unadulterated rigpa. So, at this stage, it is crucial that you settle, without suppressing or indulging thoughts, and rest repeatedly, for periods of increasing duration, in an experience of uncontrived, pure awareness. Once you have familiarized yourself with this again and again, the waves of thought will weaken and the face of rigpa you are sustaining will grow clearer. During meditation, remain in this experience for as long as you can. And in postmeditation, maintain the mindfulness of recalling the face of rigpa.

If you can familiarize yourself with this, the strength of rigpa will increase. Thoughts will continue to arise at first, but, even without your having to resort to any other remedy, they will be freed by themselves in an instant if you simply leave them as they are—just as a snake uncoils its own knots by itself. Then, with increased familiarity, rising thoughts will bring only a slight initial disturbance but will then dissolve immediately by themselves, like writing on water. As you become still more familiar with this state, you will reach a point where rising thoughts no longer have any effect at all, and you will feel neither hopeful nor anxious about their arising or nonarising. This experience of being beyond benefit and harm is likened to a thief entering an empty house.

By continuing to familiarize yourself with this practice, you will eventually reach the level of perfect strength, when thoughts and the ālaya, together with any tendency to produce movement in the mind, all dissolve into unaltered dharmakāya, and awareness is secure in its own place. Just as you might search for ordinary earth and stones on an island of gold, never to find any, at this point the whole of appearance and existence, without exception, arises as a dharmakāya realm, wherein purity is all-encompassing. This is known as gaining stability; it is the stage at which hopes and anxieties about saṃsāra and nirvāṇa or birth and death are eradicated entirely.

Just as, in this way, daytime perceptions and thoughts are gradually brought into rigpa's domain, during the nighttime too there is no need to rely on any other instruction, as this can be applied to dreams and the recognition of the clear light during both light and heavy sleep. Having understood this, persist in the practice until you gain stability, with unflagging diligence like the continuous flow of a river.

This instruction was given by Mipham. May virtue and goodness abound!

The Nature of Mind

Jamgön Mipham

Mind's nature is indivisible emptiness and clarity—
Inexpressible and indestructible, like space.
When it is seen,
there is no separate *one who sees*;
There is but a single all-encompassing sphere.
Even looker and looking are one and the same.
This view of seeing all at once is unsurpassed,
A centerless, limitless experience beyond compare.
In this fruition, when what must be done has been done,
There's no seeing at all, and any wish to see,
Any deep longing to discover the view,
Is naturally destroyed from its very depths.
To arrive at such contentment and evenness[2]
Is to be touched by brave Mañjuśrī's beneficent light.

*Mipham wrote this on the twelfth day of the seventh month, in the
year of the Fire Rat (1876). Maṅgalam!*

A Lamp to Dispel Darkness

*An Instruction That Points Directly to the Very Essence of Mind
in the Tradition of the Old Realized Ones*[3]

JAMGÖN MIPHAM

*Homage to the guru, inseparable from Mañjuśrī, the embodiment of
primordial wisdom!*

Without having to study, contemplate, or train to any great degree,
By maintaining recognition of the nature of mind according to
　　the approach of pith instructions,
Any ordinary village yogi can, without too much difficulty,
Reach the level of a vidyādhara: such is the power of this
　　profound path.

THE INSTRUCTION FOR CRACKING OPEN THE EGGSHELL OF IGNORANCE

When you leave your mind in a state of natural rest, without thinking any particular thought, and at the same time maintaining a
flow of mindfulness, you can experience a state of vacant, neutral, apathetic indifference, referred to as indeterminate, in which
consciousness is dull and blank. In this, there is none of the clear
insight of vipaśyanā, which discerns things precisely, and so the
masters call it ignorance. Since you cannot define it and say "This
is what it's like" or "This is it!" such a state is called indeterminate.
And since you cannot say what kind of state you are resting in or
what your mind is thinking, it is also called common equanimity.
In fact, you are stuck in an ordinary state within the ground-of-all
(ālaya).

Such a means of resting the mind is necessary, as a stepping-stone, in the process of bringing about nonconceptual primordial wisdom. However, as this primordial wisdom has not yet dawned, it cannot count as the main practice of Dzogchen meditation. As *The Aspiration Prayer of Samantabhadra* says:

> A blank state, devoid of any thought whatsoever—
> That is ignorance, the cause of delusion.

Therefore, when mind experiences such a dull state that lacks any thought or mental activity, allow your attention to turn naturally and gently toward the one who is aware of this state—the one who is not thinking. By doing so, you will discover the pure awareness of rigpa, free from any movement of thought, beyond any notion of outside or inside, unimpeded and open, like the clear sky. Although there is no dualistic separation here between an experience and an experiencer, still the mind is certain about its own true nature, and there is a sense that "There is nothing whatsoever beyond this." When this occurs, because you cannot conceptualize it or express it in words, it is acceptable to apply such terms as *free from all extremes, beyond description, the fundamental state of clear light,* and *the pure awareness of rigpa.*

As the wisdom of recognizing your own true nature dawns, it clears away the blinding darkness of confusion and, just as you can clearly see the inside of your home once the sun has risen, you gain confident certainty in the true nature of your mind.

This was the instruction for cracking open the eggshell of ignorance.

THE INSTRUCTION FOR CUTTING THROUGH THE WEB OF CONDITIONED EXISTENCE

When you gain this kind of realization, you understand that the nature of reality has always been so, timelessly. It is not created by any causes or conditions, and it never undergoes any kind of transition or change in the past, present, or future. At the same time, you cannot find even the tiniest fraction of something called "mind" that is separate from this nature. You could say that the state of mental blankness referred to earlier is also indescribable, but it lacks decisiveness, since you are completely *unable* to describe it in any way. Rigpa, on the other hand, is *essentially* indescribable. Yet at the same time it has a decisive quality, which cuts through any doubt about what is indescribable. There is thus a huge difference between these two kinds of indescribability, as great as the difference between blindness and perfect vision. This is also a crucial point in distinguishing between the ground-of-all and the dharmakāya. Therefore, terms such as *ordinary awareness, mental inactivity, inexpressible,* and so on are used in two different ways, only one of which is authentic. And when you know the crucial point of how the same words can have a higher level of meaning, you can gain some experience of the true meaning of the profound Dharma.

Some feel that what is to be maintained when resting naturally in the essence of mind is a simple clarity, a simple awareness, and so they settle in a state of ordinary mental consciousness, thinking, "This is clarity." Others focus their attention on an absorbing sense of emptiness, as though their minds had *become* empty. But, in both cases, there is some clinging to the dualistic experience of an aspect of ordinary mental consciousness. Whenever you find yourself in either state, look into the very nature of that subtly fixated attention—the clarity and the one perceiving the clarity, the emptiness and the one perceiving the emptiness. By doing so, you will take away the support for the ordinary consciousness that perceives things dualistically. Then, if you can decisively recognize the natural state of your own mind in all its nakedness—clear and open, without any limit or center—and a state of lucid clarity arises, that is what is called the very essence of rigpa. With this, as rigpa sheds its covering layer of experiences that involve clinging, its pure and pristine wisdom is laid bare.

This is the instruction for cutting through the web of conditioned existence.

THE INSTRUCTION FOR REMAINING IN SPACE-LIKE EQUALITY

This is how you should recognize the pure awareness of rigpa once it is freed from the various layers of ordinary thinking and experience, like a grain of rice removed from its husk—by settling naturally and making use of rigpa's own self-knowing (or self-illuminating) quality. It is not enough, however, simply to understand the nature of rigpa; you must be able to remain in that state with some stability through developing familiarity. For this, it is very important that, without becoming distracted, you sustain constant mindfulness, so as to continue resting in an utterly natural state of awareness.

When you are sustaining awareness like this, at times you might experience a vague, dull state with no thoughts, while at other times you might experience an unobstructed state with no thoughts that has the clarity of insight. At times, you might experience feelings of bliss on which you fixate, while at other times you might experience blissful feelings free of such fixation. At times, you might have various experiences of clarity involving grasping, while at other times you might experience a vivid clarity that is unsullied and free of grasping. At times, you might undergo unpleasant and unsettling experiences, while at other times you might feel pleasant and soothing sensations. And at times, you might be beset by an extreme turbulence of thought, carrying your mind away and causing you to lose your meditation. At other times, you might experience unclear states of mind because of a failure to distinguish between mental dullness and vivid clarity.

These and other experiences come about unpredictably and to an extent you cannot measure, like various waves produced by the winds of karma and habitual thoughts, cultivated throughout beginningless time. It is as though you are on a long journey, during which you visit all sorts of different places—some pleasant, some fraught with danger—but whatever happens, you must not be deterred but continue on your way.

When you are not yet familiar with this practice, and you have the experience of movement, as all manner of thoughts stir in your mind like a blazing fire, do not be discouraged. Maintain the flow of your practice without letting it slip away, and find the right balance so that you are neither too tense nor too relaxed. In this way, the more advanced meditative experiences, such as attainment,[4] will occur one after another.

At this point, investigate the distinction between the recognition and nonrecognition of rigpa, between the ground-of-all and dharmakāya, and between ordinary consciousness and wisdom. Through the master's pith instructions, and on the basis of your own personal experience, have confidence in the direct introduction you receive. While you are sustaining the essence of mind, just as water clears by itself if you do not stir it, ordinary consciousness will settle in its own nature. Focus mainly on the instructions describing how the true nature of this awareness develops into naturally arising wisdom. Do not analyze with a view to adopting one state and abandoning another, thinking, "What is this that I am cultivating in meditation? Is it ordinary consciousness or wisdom?" Nor should you entertain speculations based on an understanding derived from books, because doing so will only serve to obscure both śamatha and vipaśyanā to some degree.

At some point, the quality of familiarity with śamatha (which here means a stable continuity of mindful awareness as you settle naturally) and vipaśyanā (which here means that awareness that knows its own nature by itself) will merge automatically. When your familiarity with this becomes stable, the calm and insight that have always been inseparable, as the primordial stillness of the natural state and the clear light of your own nature, will dawn as the naturally arising wisdom that is the wisdom of the Great Perfection. This is the instruction for remaining in space-like equality.

Glorious Saraha said,

> Utterly abandon thoughts and thinking,
> And remain without thought, like a young child.

This is the way to be. He also said:

Focus on the guru's words and apply great effort—

Then, if you have received the master's instructions introducing you to your rigpa:

There is no doubt that the coemergent nature will arise.

As this says, the naturally arising wisdom that is mind's inherent nature, and which has always accompanied your ordinary mind from time immemorial, will dawn. This is no different from the inherent nature of everything, and so it is also called the actual clear light of the genuine nature.

Therefore, this approach of resting in a completely natural state and maintaining the recognition of your own self-knowing rigpa, the very essence of mind, or the dharmatā nature of phenomena, is the pith instruction that brings together a hundred crucial points in one. This is also what you are to maintain continuously.

The true measure of familiarity is the ability to maintain the state of clear light even during sleep. The signs that you are on the right track can be known through your own experience: faith, compassion, and wisdom will increase automatically, so that realization will come easily, and you will experience few difficulties. You can be certain as to the profundity and swiftness of this approach if you compare the realization it brings with that gained only through great effort in other approaches.

As a result of cultivating your mind's own natural clear light, the obscurations of ordinary thinking and the habits it creates will be naturally cleared away, and the twin aspects of omniscient wisdom will effortlessly unfold.[5] With this, as you seize the stronghold of your own primordial nature, the three kāyas will be accomplished spontaneously.

Profound! Guhya! Samaya!

This profound instruction was written by Mipham Jampel Dorje on the twelfth day of the second month in the Fire Horse year (1906), for village yogis and others who, while not able to exert themselves too much in study and contemplation, still wish to take the very essence of mind into experience through practice. It has been set out in language that is easy to understand, as raw, experiential guidance for ordinary old realized ones. Virtue! Maṅgalam!

5

A MIDLIFE CRISIS (OF ALLEGIANCE)

Jigme Tenpe Nyima was born in 1865 as the first son of the great treasure-revealer Dudjom Lingpa (1835–1904) and was soon recognized by the Fourth Dzogchen Rinpoche, Mingyur Namkhe Dorje (1793–1870), as the Third Dodrupchen incarnation. While there is no record of this recognition being contested, there are references in the biographies to an alternative identification. The biographer Delek Rabgye, for example, records that Jamyang Khyentse Wangpo believed Jigme Tenpe Nyima to be an incarnation of Gungtang Tenpe Drönme (1762–1823), an important Gelukpa scholar from Labrang Monastery. Akong Khenchen Lobzang Dorje (1893–1983) refers to this dual recognition in *The Maṇḍala of the Sun*, his extensive four-volume commentary on the *Bodhicaryāvatāra*:

> Once, when Jigme Tenpe Nyima was in discussion with his guru, Jamgön Mipham Rinpoche, the two of them used a divining mirror to determine Jigme Tenpe Nyima's previous incarnation. The mirror showed a lama wearing a yellow cloak with a black fold and a yellow preceptor's hat. In the sky above his head was the word *gung* and below his throne, *tang*.[1] At this, Mipham said, "I thought you were a rebirth of Lama Dodrup Rinpoche, but it seems you might be an incarnation of Gungtang." Staring into Jigme Tenpe Nyima's face, Mipham told him, "Well, whoever you are, while you are in this physical form, you must do all that you can for the teaching and practice of the Ancient Translation school."

Shortly after his enthronement, Jigme Tenpe Nyima traveled to Dzogchen Monastery, where he began his studies with Khenpo Pema Vajra. The biographies report that he struggled at first to understand the teachings he received. If so, he must have quickly overcome any difficulty, because in 1873, when aged just eight, he gave the annual winter lecture on the *Bodhicaryāvatāra* at Dzagyel Monastery. Afterward, Patrul Rinpoche declared that for Jigme Tenpe Nyima to have taught like that at such a young age was proof that "the period in which the Dharma of transmission will remain has not yet come to an end."

In the following years Jigme Tenpe Nyima studied with many illustrious teachers, including Patrul Rinpoche, Jamgön Mipham, the Fourth Dzogchen Rinpoche Mingyur Namkhe Dorje, Gyarong Namtrul Kunzang Tekchok Dorje, Jamyang Khyentse Wangpo, Jamgön Kongtrul Lodrö Taye, and Tertön Sogyal Lerab Lingpa. In addition, he is said to have studied the five major scriptures recognized in the Geluk tradition, as well as the debate manuals of Jamyang Shepa (1648–1721/2), with Mipham's debating opponent, Alak Dongak Gyatso.

Through these studies, Jigme Tenpe Nyima developed a reputation for the depth of his knowledge—as is evident from the autobiography of Khenpo Ngawang Palzang, which records how, on one occasion, Mipham praised both Jigme Tenpe Nyima and Tertön Sogyal as the most learned scholars in the Nyingma tradition after Nyoshul Lungtok (1829–1901). This erudition is also apparent in his own writings, which include subtle clarifications of the most difficult points of texts such as the *Bodhicaryāvatāra*, as well as two commentaries on the *Guhyagarbha Tantra* that are notorious for their difficulty.

At twenty-two, Jigme Tenpe Nyima stayed for a while with Mipham at Dzongsar Monastery. When he finally took his leave, Mipham handed him a scroll and instructed him to read it at a later date. When the time came to open it, Jigme Tenpe Nyima found that the scroll contained the verses of advice translated below. Halfway through is the statement: "If the blazing fire is not extinguished by the wind, at thirty-five, hindrances will clear and you will uphold your own lineage tradition." This was puzzling to Jigme Tenpe Nyima at first, because he felt he was already following the authentic Nyingma tradition of Longchen Rabjam and Jigme Lingpa. Still, the biographies tell us that at the predicted age he did indeed recognize the significance of Mipham's comments:

> Later, when he was thirty-five, one day, unprovoked by any cause or condition, he thought that he must study the *Eight Commands: Great Assembly of the Bliss-Gone* (*Kagye Deshek Düchen*), and he read it through entirely. This acted as a catalyst through which he realized that in the past his understanding had been influenced by the New Tradition and was not based purely on his own tradition of the Ancient Translations. He saw that there were many crucial distinctions he had not previously understood, and he felt a desire, a hundred times stronger than any he had known before, to study the texts of the Nyingma tradition. Then, from the age of about forty, it was as if the New and the Ancient reversed their positions of above and below, and he practiced only his own Nyingma tradition.[2]

Mipham was apparently satisfied with this conversion—or perhaps it is better to call it a reaffirmation—as we learn from a conversation he had with Duktsa Tulku of Dipuk, recorded in the biography written by Sönam Nyima. In a curious analogy, Mipham compares Jigme Tenpe Nyima's temporary lapse from Nyingma orthodoxy to the straying of a dog:

> Duktsa Tulku told Lama Mipham he had thought of going to see Dodrup Tulku but had decided against it. Dodrup Tulku, he said, was considered a Gelukpa, which would mean his approach diverged from their Sakya and Nyingma positions. To this, Mipham said,

"That is certainly not so. A watchdog might stray from its owner, and even forget him or her for a while, but as soon as they are reunited, the dog will recognize its master and never wander off again. Just so, Dodrup Tulku was slightly influenced by the Sarma for a time, but now he is a real Nyingmapa, I swear, and it would be good for you to visit him."[3]

The advice Mipham gave Jigme Tenpe Nyima in the scroll is a mixture of the practical and the prophetic. As is so often the case with such texts, some parts are unclear. Yet amid the more cryptic references, there are unambiguous instructions on such topics as the dangers of intellectualism ("Let go of all reliance upon tired intellectual speculation. . . . Do not settle for confused philosophical notions of what is or is not"), the real meaning of Mañjuśrī ("By resting in nonthought, you'll truly meet Mañjuśrī"), and how genuine wisdom makes teaching, writing, and other beneficial activity effortless and spontaneous. What was once a personal instruction is therefore much more than simply an obscure historical document.

Advice to the Dodrup Incarnation, Jigme Tenpe Nyima

JAMGÖN MIPHAM

With your sword, you strike the four māras at their hearts.
In your youthfulness, you are like the freshest of flowers.
The thought of you brings bliss, O deity of wisdom speech:
Be a protector now to this one who has good fortune!

Without knowing one's own situation, how can one speak of
    another's?
And yet, like a foolish father
Telling his son whatever comes to mind,
Lovingly, I say this: may you consider it always!

The tradition of the lineage is like the banks of a divine river
Kept to by those of fortune, as they avoid the routes
Suggested by the misleading words of the deceiving masses:
Hold to your own place and position, therefore, and cast away
    conceit!

When cherished philosophical ideas enter your mind,
They are hard to undermine, and you hold yourself in high regard.
Eventually, without result, you and others will be like children[4]
    roaming a desert.
You might boast, but all will be clear in the faces of those you meet.[5]

If the blazing fire is not extinguished by the wind,
At thirty-five, hindrances will clear and you'll uphold your own
    lineage tradition.[6]

Let go of various thoughts and adopt the discipline of a mendicant,
Following in the footsteps of the vidyādharas.

Let go of all reliance upon tired intellectual speculation,
From the scriptural traditions of your own and others' explanations.
And for five years meditate on instructions from the Expanse class.[7]
Then hindrances will clear and the sun of mental bliss will dawn.

Let the light of spontaneous activity blaze forth,
And let there be positive conviction in the secret of your mind.
Theory only invites further impurity, so adopt the vision of the
    practical instructions
And, without relying upon anyone else, be utterly decisive.

Look to the blissful deliverance that the king of horses brings.
Do not settle for confused philosophical notions of what is or is not,
Borne aloft at first by the noisy winds of fame and reputation.
Let the domain of wisdom be what you seek.

To take a stance and cling to a position, thinking, "This is it!"
Might seem bright enough but is like a fire of dampened wood:
It does not develop into the resolution of a great mind
But only stifles intelligence, without shedding much light.

The moon itself is pure but can appear as dim as distant stars.
All these statements come from the churning of thought.
Leave behind the analogies of foolish minds and modes of speech,
And look instead into the mind for which there can be no analogy.

When you arrive at a firm decision from within,
A hundred rainbow patterns appear effortlessly in the sky,
Unconfused and precisely distinguished.

Mañjuśrī held in thought is conceptual, confused.
But by resting in nonthought, you'll truly meet Mañjuśrī.

Now is the time to adopt the discipline of not speaking.
Do not speak, and a hundred doors to speech will open.
Speak a lot, and you will be trapped in the den of evil talk.

Neither advancing your own system nor refuting those of others,
With the discipline of an old shepherd bereft of sheep,
Let go for a time and clarity will emerge.

Be as uninhibited and free as a simpleton's soliloquy.

You might feel so confident about some lauded statement
That it yields a hundred empty explanations of supposed certainty.
But when the great gateway opens upon the dawning of naked
    wisdom,
It pours forth from within, unstoppable even if you should try.

Do not tell anyone of this—that is a sacred pledge, a samaya,
O child born as a follower of the lineage of vidyādharas!

Even though you possess the treasury of the wisdom essence,
If you take a position wherein consciousness rides the karmic
    winds,
It will create internal strife and struggle, and in the end
You'll be without accomplishment, weary, ensnared by Māra's
    emissaries.

But if you gain the warmth of bliss and awareness-wisdom,
You'll be like the lord of gods, victorious over all,
Surveying your domain with a thousand eyes, and clear in speech.

At that time, teaching, debating, composing, and acting on
    behalf of the teachings and beings
Will be effortless, accomplished spontaneously, with no difficulty
    at all.

Rely on the reverend Tārā and on Kīlaya
To liberate temporary obstacles, hindrances, and dangers.
The horse's neigh of the mighty Hayagrīva will suppress
  opposition,
And the quintessence of the peaceful and wrathful Mañjuśrī will
  dissolve into your heart.
Certainly, you should rely as well on Sitachattra.[8]
Wishes will be fulfilled and you will accomplish the twofold aim.

Do not show this to anyone else. Maṅgalam!

6

THE FINAL ROAR OF
A SCHOLAR-LION

Orgyen Tendzin Norbu (1841–1900) is something of an elusive figure in recent Nyingma history. Not much has been written about his life, and the years of his birth and death are contested. His own writings appear to have been lost, and his final testament, recorded in the few biographical accounts available, is decidedly enigmatic. Yet he was certainly important, especially in the Nyingma scholastic tradition, not least as an intermediary between his great uncle, Gyalse Shenpen Taye (1800–1855), and the foremost of his own many disciples, Shenpen Chökyi Nangwa (1871–1927). Shenpen Taye was the founder of Shri Singha, the study college at Dzogchen Monastery, and a strong proponent of monastic discipline. Shenpen Chökyi Nangwa was the founder of, and principal teacher at, several colleges, and, through his writings and teaching, helped to inspire the new scholasticism that took hold throughout Eastern Tibet in the early twentieth century. Yet Orgyen Tendzin Norbu was more than simply a human bridge linking these two prominent figures; he was also an important scholar, Dzogchen master, and teacher in his own right.

Born in Gemang Kamchung in Dzachukha in the Iron Ox Year (1841), Orgyen Tendzin Norbu entered the Shri Singha college at Dzogchen Monastery in 1853. There he took novice vows from his uncle, Shenpen Taye, who died just two years later. From the age of seventeen, he followed his main teacher, Patrul Rinpoche, for thirty years, becoming one of his principal spiritual heirs. He also studied with many others, including the Fourth Dzogchen Rinpoche Mingyur Namkhe Dorje, Khenpo Pema Vajra, Lingtrul Tupten Gyaltsen Palzang, Jamyang Khyentse Wangpo, Chokgyur

Dechen Lingpa, Tsamtrul Kunzang Tekchok Dorje, Drupchen Sönam Palge, Gemang Chöpa Jigme Tapke, and Nyoshul Lungtok. The full list of teachings that he received from these figures, but especially from Patrul Rinpoche, is strikingly long. Later he would say that while all his teachers were equal in their qualities, it was Patrul who showed him the greatest kindness.

Tulku Thondup Rinpoche notes that from 1883, when Patrul stopped taking on any more students, newcomers were directed to Orgyen Tendzin Norbu instead—and this is how Shenpen Chökyi Nangwa came to study with him. After Patrul's death, it was Orgyen Tendzin Norbu who made the funeral arrangements and who initially gathered and compiled Patrul's writings.

As a teacher, Orgyen Tendzin Norbu was tireless. While leading the simple life of a hermit—Tendzin Lungtok Nyima notes that he had no attendant and therefore boiled his own tea until the age of fifty-eight—he passed on all that he himself had received. Just like Patrul, he was especially fond of the *Bodhicaryāvatāra* and is said to have taught the text more than two hundred times in total. In addition to the major Buddhist treatises, he also lectured on grammar, poetics, medicine, astrology, and the ritual sciences. And, of course, he taught Dzogchen extensively, especially through the writings of Longchen Rabjam and Jigme Lingpa.

When Orgyen Tendzin Norbu became ill in his sixtieth year, his students reminded him that Patrul Rinpoche had lived to eighty (by Tibetan reckoning; seventy-nine by Western counting), and suggested that he should follow his guru's example for the benefit of the teachings and beings. He eventually agreed to remain for at least another thirteen days, but assured them that his commitment to the teachings and living beings would continue until the end of saṃsāra. A recent biography tells us what happened next:

> Orgyen Tendzin Norbu said, "Now, wherever I look, both by day and by night, visions of buddhas and light spheres are always present. Could they be empty forms? How amazing!" Another time, he said, "Last night, I

dreamed of a person in fine ornaments who said, 'I have come from the glorious mountain in Cāmara to collect you.' But what validity can there be to such double delusion?" A few days later, while seated before his close disciples, he gazed into the sphere of the sky, and with his right hand in the threatening gesture and his left in that of equanimity, uttered the following:

> I am Guru Padmākara of Oḍḍiyāna,
> A buddha free from birth and death.
> Awakened mind is impartial and unbiased,
> Beyond labels of the eight stages, the four pairs.

And with these final words, he passed directly to the glorious mountain of Cāmara.[1]

At first glance, what is most striking about this testament is its bold assertion—"the lion's roar," as Jigme Tenpe Nyima calls it—in the first two lines. But equally remarkable, and what sets it apart from other testaments of this kind, is the reference to the eight stages in the final line. These are the four categories of stream enterer, once returner, nonreturner, and arhat, each of which can be further divided into emerging and established, giving eight stages in total. For such a decidedly scholastic reference—a taxonomy from the Abhidharma—to appear alongside a declaration of Dzogchen realization is certainly unusual, if not actually unique.[2]

The following text, entitled "Advice in Response to the Request of the Faithful, Diligent, and Intelligent Deshul Drakden," is Dodrupchen Jigme Tenpe Nyima's brief commentary on Orgyen Tendzin Norbu's final words. It shows how the four lines are more than just a declaration of Dzogchen's superiority, as they also convey an instruction for the moment of death. This makes Orgyen Tendzin Norbu's final words an apt reflection of his life: dedicated, as it was, not only to extensive study and practice but, above all, to guiding others—even until its very last moment.

Advice in Response to the Request of the Faithful, Diligent, and Intelligent Deshul Drakden

Jigme Tenpe Nyima

Homage to the guru!

Our noble teacher, Orgyen Tendzin Norbu, trained in the five sciences and gained liberation through the Great Perfection's path of the Heart Essence. At the time of his passing, he spoke the following verse as his final testament:

> I am Guru Padmākara of Oḍḍiyāna,
> A buddha free from birth and death.
> Awakened mind is impartial and unbiased,
> Beyond labels of the eight stages, the four pairs.

I shall elaborate a little on the meaning of this.

Generally, all the various turnings of the wheel of Dharma by the Lord Buddha were offered purely to protect disciples from the miserable routine of birth, death, and the intermediate state. Among these teachings, for the ultimate tradition of the Heart Essence, which is the vajra pinnacle, there is no delusion in the condition of great primordial purity, the original ground. And yet, because we do not recognize this, appearances of delusion, which are the creative energy of rigpa, arise. Through the three types of ignorance—seeming identity, coemergent, and imputational—thoughts involving dualistic grasping develop, one after another, in an endless chain. Then, through grasping, we are drawn into the endless cycle of suffering caused by karma and mental afflictions. Recognizing and becoming familiar with the actual nature of the essence, which is untainted by confusion, naturally averts the delusions of birth and death. Yet we cannot see the nature of this essence through intellectual speculation or through a mind that is contrived. Instead, we must receive the nectar of ripening empowerments and liberating instructions from an authentic guru who has inherited the actual transmission. Then, by cultivating the devotion of seeing the guru as inseparable from the Vajradhara of Oḍḍiyāna, our mind will be inspired with blessings, and the guru's wisdom mind will merge inseparably with our own mind. Through this, we will recognize the mind's natural condition, without contrivance or contamination, as the all-perfect, death-less Padmākara himself. We must then firmly decide that this is so and gain stability. As this recognition is not generated through temporary causes and conditions, it is free from birth. And as it is not seen to increase or decrease or undergo transition or change, it is free from death. Thus, the attainment of birthlessness and death-lessness is bestowed naturally, there and then. And when we gain the confidence of not seeking buddhahood elsewhere, there can be the lion's roar proclaiming:

I am Guru Padmākara of Oḍḍiyāna,
A buddha free from birth and death.

When the nature of this awareness or awakening mind manifests, appearances of birth and death are cast aside, the mind of fixated clinging is cut from within, and the cycle of conceptualization is left behind.

Hopes and fears, or notions of adopting and avoiding, focused on a nirvāṇa that is beyond conceptual elaboration, do not bring about any fragmentation of pure awareness, which is itself unsup-ported. Rather, whatever appears is its natural self-appearance, and whatever arises does so as its self-expression. All that might be labeled as subjective or objective throughout saṃsāra and nirvāṇa simply arises as the evolving manifestation of this pure awareness that is itself beyond partiality and bias. And these expressions dissolve within the ground. Once the stronghold of the ground is seized in its own place, this is superior to the original ground, as there is awakening within the sphere of the dharmakāya, the youthful vase body, clear light beyond confinement and restriction. Thus, the testament says:

Awakened mind is impartial and unbiased.

Therefore, in this vehicle there is no system of positing the fruition as something separate, as there is for the eight stages of the four pairs. According to that approach, we regard delusory appearances as faults and train in a limited form of yoga, through which it is possible to overcome the "seeing discards" of the three realms, but not the "meditation discards" of the desire realm; or else, to enter that realm in order to discard them; or to discard most of the desire-realm afflictions; or to discard them all but not totally overcome the afflictions related to the two upper realms, with the result that the sufferings of birth and death are still not entirely overcome, and so on. Here, by contrast, out of the expanse of realization of great, all-pervasive primordial purity, which is self-appearing and unbiased, all grounds and paths are traversed at once. This point must be spelled out in detail, so the testament says:

Beyond labels of the eight stages, the four pairs.

This also shows how Dzogchen is superior to the lower vehicles.

The meaning in a nutshell, then, is as follows. Merging your own mind inseparably with the guru's wisdom, settle evenly—without deliberately *settling*—in the genuine expanse of rigpa-emptiness. Then, at death, none of the terrifying delusory appearances of the intermediate state will cause awareness to stray from its own place. This "seizing of the stronghold" is the essential message of the first three lines. It is the ultimate instruction for the moment of death within this tradition and is also known as the *ultimate dharmakāya transference through sealing with the view*. For this, there is much to understand, such as the way to sustain it right now, as well as the way to apply it at the time of death.

The final line shows how this path is superior to the other vehicles, all of which require effort; it means that certainty in one's own path must be stable.

To put it another way: The first two lines show the means of achieving deathlessness through this path. Still, some might object that this alone would not make this the pinnacle of vehicles, because even the śrāvakas and pratyekabuddhas have a path that puts a stop to the sufferings of birth and death. In that case, it would suffice to offer the final line as a response and the third line as the reason.

In response to persistent requests from the faithful, diligent, and intelligent Deshul Drakden, Tenpe Nyima quickly wrote down whatever came to mind on the third excellent day of the waning phase [i.e., the twenty-seventh] of the Phālguna month in the Earth Bird Year (1909).

7

A LITTLE LEARNING IS A
DANGEROUS THING

When Jigme Tenpe Nyima wrote the text that I am calling (with apologies to William Hazlitt) "On the Ignorance of the Learned,"[1] he was not making a strikingly original point. There was nothing new about the view that intellectualism can be a pitfall on the path, and warnings of its dangers are commonplace throughout Tibetan literature. Indeed, the notion that book learning is merely superficial, while it is meditation that brings about genuine and lasting wisdom, is an ancient one. In Tibetan literature, this dichotomy takes dramatic form in the familiar trope of the scholarly geshe being outwitted (and possibly humiliated) by a simple yogi—best exemplified in Milarepa's encounters with the arrogant, scheming Geshe Tsakpuwa.

Yet, if there was a change in the nineteenth and early twentieth centuries, it was that schools such as the Nyingma and Kagyü, which had traditionally been associated with tantric adepts and meditating hermits like Milarepa, began to accommodate large-scale scholasticism. These schools had produced their own great scholars in the past, but widespread monastic education of the kind introduced through the establishment of study colleges was something new. And it meant that what had long been a characteristic of other traditions—memorization of treatises, formal debate, and so on—was increasingly a feature within their own traditions as well.[2]

Jigme Tenpe Nyima studied Buddhist philosophical topics, including the Middle Way, transcendent perfection of wisdom (*prajñāpāramitā*), and Abhidharma, with khenpos trained in the Geluk system. He was even taught by Mipham's erstwhile opponent, Alak Dongak Gyatso. The form of education he received emphasizes logic and debate. And, in the long term, this training seemingly stood him in good stead, for his writings demonstrate remarkable clarity and precision, even when the topic is Tantra or Dzogchen. Still, the colophon to "On the Ignorance of the Learned" tells us that he wrote the text from personal experience. This might mean that he initially fell victim to the kind of unhealthy intellectualism he describes, which Patrul Rinpoche calls "the demon of excessive learning."[3] Or, if he was not subject to this himself—and he does also claim, somewhat unconvincingly, that his own education was minimal—he might at least have witnessed it in others.

In addition to listing the dangers of intellectualism, Jigme Tenpe Nyima's text also offers definitions of what it means to be truly learned or wise from a Buddhist perspective. Unsurprisingly, genuine learning turns out to be more a matter of integrating and embodying the instructions than collecting or even memorizing them. As a well-known saying puts it, "The sign of true learning is a peaceful temperament. The mark of meditation is a reduction in the mental afflictions." The kind of intellectual Jigme Tenpe Nyima describes has a mind that is far from peaceful, as it restlessly rehearses arguments and frantically searches for faults in everything. Such a scholar is an example of what Tibetans call a *togewa*, a sophist or logician who cannot transcend the intellectual realm—who is, we might almost say, incurably pedantic.

On the Ignorance of the Learned

Jigme Tenpe Nyima

The precious teaching collections of the Omniscient Guide are Dharma teachings that we should learn; they are the fundamental scriptures with which we should become acquainted. For bodhisattvas, studying these texts brings an increase in the causes of all-seeing wisdom and mastery of the methods for bringing those of diverse inclinations to spiritual maturity.

Nevertheless, there are some these days who pursue study and yet the more they learn, the more arrogant they become. They think, "Now I have studied widely. I know the scriptural approach. I am learned in the various collections." And when they see others who have not amassed comparable learning, they regard them with contempt, thinking, "These people are fools, dullards, simpletons, befuddled, uneducated." Even when reading texts by fellow scholars, they lack due reverence and devotion for the sacred Dharma. No sooner have they opened the covers of a book than they are wondering, "What have we here? How is this written?" As unstable in their understanding as if their intelligence were laid out on a bed of reeds, they point their fingers accusingly and gesticulate like drunkards. Encountering a claim, they think, "This does not accord with the Pramāṇa texts on logic and epistemology." Confronted with another assertion, they say to themselves, "This does not fit with what is taught in the Abhidharma." Reading of some further proposition, they decide, "Oh, this can be refuted by such and such a line of thinking." Critiquing in such a way, they reach the end of the text with no clear idea of what it contains or maintains, no notion of what it asserts or posits.

Such scholars think, "When others debate with my system, they will say such and such, so I must reply as follows. . . . But then the opponent might counter with such and such a response, so what would be the best reply?" Constantly preoccupied with such thoughts, they feel no pleasure during the day, and sleep evades them at night. Even if sleep should come, as they are consumed by such matters even in their dreams, their minds will be perturbed from the very first moment of waking. Dismissing the works of the profound path, including the progressive stages of meditation on bodhicitta and compassion, as too easy to understand, they prefer works of sophistry. And whenever they come across such books they think, "Oh, now this I must study!" As they open a volume, they immediately muster all their intellect and ask such questions as "What is the meaning of this? Now this is a mere illustration. Is this a refutation? Is this a valid proof? Does this follow logically from the premise? Is there a logical contradiction here?" Scribbling notations about hairsplitting points, they pass the best part of the afternoon, their pulse racing, their breath uneven.

From the very moment that you focus on such topics as the "conceptual isolate" of the Buddha or the "substance universal" of sentient beings, all faith and renunciation diminish and disappear. Eventually, at the time of your death, all that you have studied will be shown to be nothing but dry, empty words, all your analysis and research amounting to no more than hollow ideas, and all that you have read garnering little more than false suppositions—all based on squandered opportunities. It is then plainly apparent that all this analysis and categorizing into matter, consciousness, and anomalous factors is nothing more than casting stones in the dark.

If you think about it, you will see that the path of logic is intended to dispel incorrect patterns of thought. Yet once such patterns have been dispelled, it is necessary to set out upon the genuine path and, having set out upon this path, to make manifest the wisdom of perfect liberation.

To be learned in the Dharma does not mean merely to have heard a lot of teachings. "The one who, because of learning, feels disenchantment for the three realms—such a person is *truly* learned," says the Abhidharma. One ought, therefore, to examine any pretensions of learning based on knowing a few facts about this or that. *The Sūtra Requested by Bhadramāyākāra* teaches that the essence of being learned is to practice whatever Dharma you have heard and to benefit others by explaining it to them well. So we must be wary of presuming to uphold the lifestyle of the learned while pursuing only a limited, superficial approach to logical reasoning bereft of such meaningful objectives.

Although my own education resembles nothing more than the watery traces of a silkworm upon a lotus, I have some experience in these matters, and so I, the crazy beggar Jigme, offer this mad talk for those who might be in a similar position.

8

REMEMBRANCE OF
AWARENESS PRESENT

Jigme Tenpe Nyima seems to have taken a particular interest in memory. Among his best-known works is *An Explanation of Dhāraṇī*, on the mnemonic powers of bodhisattvas, a text widely praised for its originality. (Amdo Geshe Jampal Rolwe, for instance, called it an "unsurpassed wonder," while his foremost student, Dongak Chökyi Gyatso, eulogized it in a series of verses.)[1] And in his writings on the Great Perfection too, Jigme Tenpe Nyima often refers to memory in the specific sense of *remembering* the pure awareness introduced by the teacher. In fact, some instructions describe the path of *trekchö* as little more than a process of remembering rigpa—or, to put it another way, remaining undistracted from rigpa. Although we might term this mindfulness, it is not mindfulness as the term is generally understood in other (lower) forms of Buddhism. Indeed, Dzogchen distinguishes its own brand of uncontrived, natural mindfulness from what it considers to be the artificial, unnatural mindfulness cultivated through lower forms of meditation. Deliberately holding an object in mind and paying attention to it can be compared to hanging a coat on a peg, these teachings say: the object and what holds it in place are separate, brought together only through circumstances. In the Great Perfection, by contrast, mindfulness is understood as a property of pure awareness itself, as intrinsic as heat is to fire.

There are various terms used to describe or characterize the Dzogchen form of mindfulness (or memory): innate, genuine, transcending the ordinary mind, supreme, sovereign, effortless, naturally present. But these are all means of distinguishing the mindfulness of the Great Perfection from the mindfulness of the lower levels of the teaching, which is thus understood to be artificial, false, part of the ordinary mind, inferior, lowly, effortful, and contrived.

The text translated below, which Jigme Tenpe Nyima wrote for a student called Gyurme Dorje,[2] does not simply highlight the qualities of mindfulness in the Great Perfection; it explains how this mindfulness develops on the path. Expanding upon a verse from Longchen Rabjam's *Treasury of Pith Instructions*—a text that consists entirely of sixfold classifications—Jigme Tenpe Nyima identifies six stages in the development of Dzogchen mindfulness. The progression begins with something more deliberate. But after the first stage the practice becomes simpler and more natural: a gradual strengthening of familiarity with the mindful quality that is intrinsic to pure awareness. This development continues until the final stage, when all ordinary phenomena are said to dissolve within the natural state of dharmatā. As Jigme Tenpe Nyima makes clear, the more advanced states of realization might be said to include memory or mindfulness of rigpa in the sense that there is a continuous abiding by pure awareness, but, as he also points out, this is quite unlike what we might ordinarily understand by such terms.

Advice for the
Devoted Student Gyurme Dorje

Jigme Tenpe Nyima

From the oceanic treasury of stainless knowledge
Flow the river-like teachings of the aural lineage,
The mighty waters of the supreme vajra vehicle—
Khyentse Özer, at your feet I bow!

Here I shall offer an essential summary of the key points of the view
and meditation of the definitively secret Great Perfection, present-
ing them in the context of the six forms of mindfulness. This has
two parts: a general summary and a detailed explanation.

GENERAL SUMMARY

The omniscient guru said:

> Beginners achieve nondistraction through deliberate
> application.
> Students of meditation and postmeditation are naturally
> undistracted.
> Familiarity brings nondistraction as perceptions dawn as
> wisdom.
> With expansive realization, there is no distraction nor one
> who is distracted.
> With ultimate stability, what were objects of distraction are
> assuredly dharmatā,
> And, with phenomenal dissolution, illustrations or
> expressions no longer apply.

DETAILED EXPLANATION

This has six sections: (1) applied mindfulness, (2) natural mindfulness, (3) mindfulness during postmeditative experience, (4) mindfulness of direct realization, (5) mindfulness encompassing experience, and (6) the mindfulness of phenomenal dissolution.

Applied Mindfulness

This is equivalent to the first of the three modes of liberation the great master Vimalamitra described: liberation through recognizing thought, which is compared to meeting an old acquaintance. In this regard, if you have already practiced the general generation phase of Unsurpassed Secret Mantra, there is no need to cultivate śamatha separately. Still, this should not be taken to imply that the perfection phase can only ever be practiced on the basis of the generation phase. After all, it is well known that in this tradition of the king of vehicles clear light is made manifest through the pursuit of naked, primordially pure awareness alone.

Moreover, there are some whose minds are unsuited to samādhi because of the prominent movement of thought. They cannot swiftly distinguish the ordinary mind from the pure awareness of rigpa within their own experience. This is because rigpa is the most rarefied aspect of mind and awareness and is extremely difficult to lay bare in a mind that is disturbed. It is therefore crucially important that right at the outset, before sustaining the essence of rigpa, you look directly into the essence of mind.

To distinguish among stillness, movement, and awareness, *movement* refers to any subtle or coarse level of thought, whether good or bad, belonging to the category of mental profusion. *Stillness* means the absence of dullness and agitation in an essentially clear, penetrating mind. And *awareness* is that which notices whether movement has overtaken the mind as it sustains the flow of stillness.

Furthermore, both focusing your attention when it is scattered and allowing concentrated thought to disperse into agitation are considered hindrances to samādhi. You must therefore allow all movement, good and bad, to subside calmly and gently within the experience of stillness. For this, instructions on dispelling hindrances, such as bringing out the clarity of mind whenever it is dull, or looking directly into the essence of mind whenever it is agitated, are extremely important. Otherwise, a subtle dullness of mind can intensify, leading to ordinary śamatha and only strengthening delusion.

In short, pure samādhi, with the kind of mental pliancy required to focus on any given object, means maintaining an awareness that is untainted by any of the faults of meditative concentration, such as laziness, dullness, or agitation, without letting it slip away. The most important means of sustaining such a state is to remain in an experience of mind's own essence without allowing it to be lost. And for such a method, we must settle primarily through mindfulness (or remembering). What it means to be mindful—or not pass beyond the bounds of mindfulness—in this context is that you do not lose the essence of mind.

The term *applied* is used because when meditating there is no reduction of effort in samādhi—and that alone is at the very heart of the practice. This then is what we call *applied mindfulness.*

Natural Mindfulness

When the mind is made pliable through applied mindfulness, the practitioner takes as the path the pure awareness of rigpa, which is beyond the ordinary mind. This is based on the second mode of liberation from the approach of the Natural Great Perfection, the instruction on liberating thoughts just as a snake uncoils its own knots. At this stage, any intellectual speculation or form of analytical meditation on emptiness would prove insufficient by itself. Instead, everything must be brought together and integrated into this, the ultimate of all swift paths for attaining enlightenment. Of course, it is true that there could be no greater *object* of meditative equipoise than the emptiness in which all things are eliminated—down to their flesh and bones, as it were. Nevertheless, the Unsurpassed level of Vajrayāna is vastly superior in its methods for settling. It says in a tantra:

> Because of which, through sacred bliss,
> You will gain supreme accomplishment in this very life.

As this indicates, once the natural, coemergent primordial liberation, the very state of the Original Protector, is made manifest, each moment can bring the equivalent of many aeons of ordinary accumulation. It is only the works of the Great Perfection that teach the uncommon aspects of the supreme, unchanging wisdom, as it is universally known in the second (i.e., perfection) phase of Unsurpassed Mantra. And it is only these same texts that teach the means of making this wisdom manifest, treating the practice of pursuing naked awareness—and naked awareness alone—as the most important of practices from the very moment you set out on the path of Unsurpassed Mantra. Having understood the key point of the path, therefore, we must take it into our experience.

The actual means of bringing this about is to take as the main practice the pure awareness to which the guru introduced us in the past. As we settle evenly into an experience of this awareness, without fabrication or contrivance, even if all dualistic thoughts do not fade into all-pervading space right away, they will be rendered ineffective. It is rather like someone afflicted with a severe illness—no matter how much you might show them arrays of brightly colored silk, their mind will be so oppressed by suffering that they will have no thought of looking. Just so, the mind's ordinary mode of apprehension will be so overwhelmed by the features of clear light that it will experience only vivid clarity.

Furthermore, what we call "sustaining the flow of awareness" does not involve identifying with the wisdom introduced by the guru. Nor does it mean thinking about the way in which the introduction was effected. Rather, it means recognizing the ultimate point at which the eighty conceptualizations and the karmic winds, together with any habitual tendencies, dissolve, and then remaining without losing that recognition. This alone is the very cornerstone of all forms of trekchö meditation.

The mindfulness of not losing the essence of pure awareness, as just described, is called natural mindfulness (literally, the mindfulness of dharmatā). The key to this is as follows. There are many occasions in multiple tantras when the term "ultimate truth of clear light" is used. Yet, until genuine clear light is seen, the union of awareness and emptiness is not perfected, and this term refers to what has always been, in its essence, inexpressible emptiness and clarity. Here too, by the same logic, there can be distinctions in what is labeled *dharmatā*, just as we speak of sixteen types of emptiness, where the distinctions relate to the bases of emptiness—that is, the things that are empty—rather than emptiness itself. The mode of emptiness is just as explained in the texts on the Middle Way. But since the basis of emptiness here is rigpa, we can consider its emptiness special, just as sentient beings and noble buddhas are equally empty but, owing to the difference in their respective bases for emptiness, buddhas are said to be svabhāvikakāya, while beings are not. Therefore, as this stage involves the mindfulness of not losing an experience of the intrinsic nature of this basis of emptiness, which is the mind of clear light, it is referred to as natural (or dharmatā) mindfulness.

Mindfulness during Postmeditative Experience

At this stage, you not only sustain the essence of awareness during meditative equipoise, in the manner just explained, but practice this in postmeditation too. This means you recognize how all forms of mental elaboration, including the objects of the six senses and perceptions related to them, are all primordially pure. In other words, you are certain that these phenomena arise as the creative expression of awareness, and yet never stray from the genuine kāya of the ground of liberation, the mind of clear light, or Samantabhadra.

The second Omniscient One, Jigme Lingpa, spelled out how to bring the infinite purity of the radiance of spontaneous perfection onto the path in his answers to questions on meditation. Here, it is just as Lhatsün, the lord of ḍākinīs,[3] says:

I am a yogi of the Great Perfection,
Realizing all phenomena to be naked awareness.

If you understand the key point in this way, then the path of trekchö in the Great Perfection essentially boils down to an understanding of how appearances and perceptions are liberated in the ground. Everything that appears in this world, be it animate or inanimate, originates from karma, and the root of karma is mind. Candrakīrti explains this point, as well as how mind is the most important factor in the three realms, in his commentary to *Introduction to the Middle Way*. Such accounts serve as a foundation. Still, going further, we must understand that the mind, which is the most important factor in the three realms, is mounted upon wind energy. And ultimately the activity of generating and absorbing all this wind energy is as explained in *The Blazing Charnel Ground Heap*:[4]

The essence of mind is wisdom,
To which dualistic perception arises as its creative expression.

As this indicates, the ultimate owner of the mind, or basis for its generation, is said to be the wisdom of clear light. If you explain precisely how everything comes down to pure awareness itself, it exposes the deceit of most foolish meditators today—those who only feign realization, who believe that ultimately the significance of rigpa's expressive power involves nothing more than avoiding such terrible crimes as putting men to the sword and women to the spear.

The practice, then, is to transform all that you experience and perceive during postmeditation into the yoga of recognizing rigpa's expressions as illusory. If you can maintain an experience of mindfulness that is imperturbable and all-pervasive, it will also become a support for inspiring rigpa during meditation. The way in which this works is very clearly explained not only in Dzogchen's own tantras but also in the Mahāyoga tantras and the commentaries on their intention.

Mindfulness of Direct Realization

The three modes of liberation relate to the stage of meditating on the Great Perfection; they do not explain the stage of realization. The inconceivable awareness of the Great Perfection is, therefore, clear light that is entirely free not only from the marks of conceptuality but also even from the three illuminating experiences. This is the view of the omniscient Jigme Lingpa, the great pioneering commentator on this king of vehicles. In *Training in the Pure Realms of the Three Kāyas*, he explains how the three illuminating experiences arise and then immediately follows this with a description of the features of ultimate clear light:

> In this moment, may I realize the primordial purity of the
>   present, the space that is free from conceptual mind,
> As "ordinary" awareness, fresh, vast, and boundless.
> And through the power of gaining certainty and meditating
>   in such a state,
> In that very instant may I seize the stronghold
> Of the space of the primordial ground, the secret depth of
>   inner luminosity,
> The vast expanse of youthful vase body, endowed with its six
>   special qualities!

This is an explanation of what is beyond description. The dawning of clear light referred to here is necessarily identical to direct realization in the Great Perfection. And this cannot occur until the wind energies enter the central channel. As the Omniscient One said:

> With the karmic winds of dualistic perception inside the
> central channel,
> In the Great Perfection, there is no notion that they could
> lead one astray.[5]

This refers to the stage that begins when the wind energies enter
the central channel with very little force. In the main practice of
meditation, the karmic winds and the movement of thought that
is dependent upon them are naturally brought to a halt. The three
modes of liberation are therefore means of sustaining the practice
when thoughts have not yet disappeared.

Direct seeing in the Great Perfection occurs from Dzogchen's
own path of joining onward, while Dzogchen meditation begins
on the path of accumulation. Some so-called great meditators have
not so much as glimpsed even the general tendency of this vajra
path. They have no idea that settling without accepting or rejecting
thoughts, which generally comes later, brings about the warmth
that usually occurs earlier. To such practitioners, even talk of the
crucial point of thoughts fading into basic space will seem bizarre,
like seeing a white crow for the very first time. Still, I shall persist,
as untroubled as a madman striking a yak on the nose.

What we are concerned with here corresponds to the line,
"With expansive realization, there is no distraction nor one who
is distracted." This means that when we see the mind of clear light
vividly and clearly in the Great Perfection, the six sensory objects
that are potential sources of distraction and the dualistic perception that could be distracted are no more. They have disappeared
entirely within great natural clarity, following the dissolution of
the karmic winds. That is the real sense of this line, not some form
of stability that must be protected from distraction.

As long as there is movement of wind energy, the actual face of
pure awareness will be obscured during meditative equipoise by
the thoughts and three illuminating experiences that are rigpa's
expression. And therefore, as long as practitioners do not neglect
the natural resting place of experience, they will not stray from the

vajra-like nature of the mind. Although we might term this *mind-fulness*, you must understand that it is not at all like lesser ways of being mindful.

Mindfulness Encompassing Experience

The fifth stage corresponds to the fusing together of the power of the practice of meditative equipoise and experiences during post-meditation. This means there is an emphasis on the experience of realization, in which appearance and awareness arise as the radiance of clear light. There is some similarity here with the third stage described above. However, that type of mindfulness was a means of sustaining experience between sessions, when meditating on the essence of pure awareness. By contrast, this is a way of integrating postmeditative appearances from the point when rigpa can be elicited through the force of experience. So, just as there is a great difference in the power of your practice based on whether the wind energies have entered the central channel during meditation, in postmeditative experience too there is a vast difference in how this power is integrated.

Mindfulness of Phenomenal Dissolution

Addendum: The Vast Expanse of Space,[6] which presents the five paths in the Great Perfection, explains that this form of mindfulness comes about once the realization of the path of seeing has been made manifest. This could be interpreted in very different ways, based on whether it is the Great Perfection more generally that is seen or not seen, or the profound dharmatā, which is the spontaneously perfect rigpa of the Great Perfection. While the former can occur at the path of joining, the latter occurs only from the path of seeing. Although this kind of explanation of the five paths is rather imprecise, it is extremely simple. Even so, these days there are very few for whom this level of the union of rigpa and emptiness arises in the mind. As the pure awareness of clear light is untainted by any deluded thought, the term *sky-like* can be applied even at the earlier stage. Nevertheless, it is only at the later stage that we reach the essence of wisdom in which even the slightest trace of dualistic perception has faded into inconceivable emptiness beyond any extreme. And this makes the later stage uniquely beyond illustration and expression. An extensive presentation of these points can be found in the inexhaustible collections of works by the omniscient kings of Dharma, Longchen Rabjam and Jigme Lingpa, and their followers, but I shall say no more here.

In general, if you hold the position that there is a difference between the "dissolution of phenomena" as one of the four visions and what it means here, then the stage of rigpa reaching full measure—one of the four visions—must also be included here. But if you consider that there is no difference, then you should know that rigpa reaching full measure and the final experience of "the sphere of precious spontaneous accomplishment" must be grouped together.

Thus, these lines (of the original verse by Longchenpa) encapsulate how to accomplish śamatha in the beginning, how to cultivate clear light in the middle, how the Great Perfection arises at the end, and how its fruition is attained. In other words, they include both the path and fruition of this, the king of all vehicles.

This talk of the sovereign, supreme, and wondrous vehicle
Is like the merest droplet among drops of dew,
The tiniest fragment among fragments—
Still, may it inspire all the world to practice virtue!

As a reply to the devoted student Gyurme Dorje, the beggar Jigme wrote down whatever arose in his mind during a tea break. May it prove virtuous and auspicious!

9

A Portrait of the Master as a Young Tulku

At some point in his life, although exactly when is unclear, Jigme Tenpe Nyima suddenly became seriously ill. The biographer Sönam Nyima claims that he was targeted by an evil spirit (formerly a wicked minister), who had also plagued his father, Dudjom Lingpa. One day, when Jigme Tenpe Nyima was teaching, a violent storm descended, and as soon as he was touched by the wind, he could hardly move. Thereafter, it was his brother, Pema Dorje, who took charge of the monastery, while Jigme Tenpe Nyima retired to a hermitage, where he remained in ill health for the rest of his life. Although he sometimes taught at the hermitage, it became notoriously difficult to meet him directly. Those who did wish to see him often went to great lengths to do so. Akong Khenpo Lobzang Dorje, for instance, became a scribe, copying texts for the private library, before undertaking a one-year retreat, all so that he could receive teachings and empowerments from the master.

Still, while most prospective students were denied access to Jigme Tenpe Nyima in his hermitage, there were exceptions. Among the most notable was Jamyang Khyentse Chökyi Lodrö, who in 1920 spent several months with Jigme Tenpe Nyima, receiving empowerments and instructions. Jigme Tenpe Nyima was especially generous with the incarnation of one of his principal gurus, sharing a great number of teachings and much advice. At the end of their meeting he entrusted the young tulku with all his writings, encouraging him to study and transmit them.

The text that follows does not mention Jamyang Khyentse Chökyi Lodrö by name, but there is no doubt that he was the correspondent whose twenty-four questions on the Great Perfection

Jigme Tenpe Nyima answers. He is the "noble lord" whose studies Jigme Tenpe Nyima encourages and the aspiring Dzogchen master for whom he provides what amounts to a list of required reading. Still, it is less clear exactly when these letters were sent. Jamyang Khyentse was evidently still quite young, but does this mean that the text predates his journey to Dodrupchen in 1920? Possibly, but as the questions also demonstrate more than a passing familiarity with Dzogchen theory and practice, it is equally possible they were sent some time thereafter.

In any case, whatever the date of its composition, the work that follows offers a fascinating glimpse behind the scenes—behind the closed door of the hermitage, as it were—revealing something of the intimate process of transmission. The text itself is in fact part of that process. Jamyang Khyentse Chökyi Lodrö would, of course, go on to become one of the most highly respected and revered teachers of the twentieth century, but here we see him as an inquisitive student. And though Jigme Tenpe Nyima had already gained a reputation as one of the most learned and accomplished scholars of recent times, here we see him sharing his wisdom and guidance with the utmost humility. Even leaving aside its extraordinary subject matter, what follows is therefore no ordinary Q&A.

Answers to Questions
on the Great Perfection

JIGME TENPE NYIMA

Namo guru!

Although it is difficult for the likes of me, so deficient in intellect, to respond accurately to the several questions on the Great Perfection that you, noble lord, recently wrote and passed on to me, still I offer the following hasty, partial answers.

1. We can understand from the works of the Great Perfection that there is a ground of liberation—one of two aspects of the ground itself, which is divided into a ground of delusion and a ground of liberation. To claim that the ground of delusion is spontaneously present in the ground of liberation would be tantamount to asserting that the ground is flawed. So, is the ground of delusion temporary or not?

The great Brahmin Saraha said:

> Mind-as-such alone is the seed of all,
> Wherein conditioned existence and nirvāṇa arise.

As this indicates, if the genuine mind of clear light alone is not recognized, then it is the ground of delusion; whereas if it is recognized and stability is attained, it becomes the source of liberation. As the former corresponds to the phase of the ground and the latter to the phase of fruition, the great Omniscient One refuted claims that these two are identical. At the ground stage, every time we die, the clear light dawns in its entirety, but, through our failure to recognize it, we revert to the flow of deluded, dualistic grasping. By contrast, when we arrive at the state of liberation, there can be no turning back, because the stronghold has been seized directly. This is the difference.

At the ground stage, we do not recognize our own essence, so the ground of delusion is set in place through speculation about the spontaneous expressions arising through confusion. We can see that this is not the inherent condition of the genuine nature of clear light itself. If it were, then the more we recognized the essence or perfected its strength, the more the deluded experiences of saṃsāric existence would increase. We do not assert, therefore, that the basis of delusion and the ground of liberation are the same, nor do we accept that the clear light of the ground, which is believed to be the basis for delusion, is a temporary phenomenon. It seems to me that such views would be like attempts to draw a sharp distinction between primordial purity and spontaneous presence.

2. If delusion is not present in the ground itself but involves clinging to its expressions—the manifestations of the ground—as good or bad, does the combination of wind energy and mind, which is the one who is deluded, exist separately?

The clear light of the ground never develops into the essence of delusion; it could not possibly do so, which is why it is described as primordially liberated, utterly pure from the beginning, alpha pure, and so on. But then we cannot say that the wind energy and mind, which has begun to cling to ground appearances, is undeluded. Therefore, we must say that these two are not identical and are distinct. Still, as was said by the awareness holders of the past, although delusion is not clear light, there would be no delusion were it not for clear light. In view of this, I wonder if we should not assert that delusion is of the same nature or essence as clear light but differs in substance.

3. When there is delusion about dharmakāya, primordial wisdom, and pure awareness, they turn into the ground-of-all, ordinary consciousness, and ordinary mind. The former three are said to be beyond bondage and liberation and lacking in any concrete identity—being limitless and free from partiality or bias—yet capable of taking on any form, as shown through the analogy of a mirror in which various reflections can arise. So, what is the key to the arising of sentient beings for whom saṃsāra does not merely appear, but who are bound through deluded attachment?

When we speak of "the stirring of ground appearance from the ground," ground appearance does not refer only to visionary appearances such as buddha forms, lights, and light spheres. It also refers to all that unfolds through the outward radiance of compassionate energy's awareness. Through this expression or force, just as tarnish appears on gold or algae develops in water, an adventitious form of consciousness develops in which objects appear to be distinct from the perceiving subject. When this first develops in a subtle form, it is termed *ground-of-all*. Then, as wind energy and mind become more coarse, the six senses and the defiled mind emerge. The major works of the Great Perfection discuss this process in detail when describing how sentient beings fail to realize the ground and become deluded.

Therefore, since actual pure awareness is primordially pure, it does not develop the features of reifying attachment. Rather, it is the coarser states of mind, which arise out of this pure awareness, that develop into the reifying attachment of ordinary beings. From this, it is easy to understand the subsequent stages of the process and the development of compositional karma, sentient beings, and the various realms of sentient beings.

4. Do the dissolution phases of appearance, increase, and attainment arise during the first bardo of dying for those who are strong in the practices of "blending the three spaces" and transference?

I think the phases of dissolution must arise in any such instance. Liberation through entering the sphere of clear light is for those who attain stability during the clear light of death, and that clear light must be preceded by the occurrence of the dissolution phase. Then there are those who are liberated through the ejection and transference of consciousness and who are transported to a pure realm once consciousness has left the body. In such cases, the departure of consciousness occurs only after the clear light of death, which itself occurs after the dissolution process.

5. What is the difference between the phase of consciousness dissolving into appearance (and the rest) and the phase of consciousness dissolving into space?

If the dissolution of consciousness into space is further subdivided, it consists of the dissolution of consciousness into appearance, then of appearance into increase, and so on, so they are essentially the same.

6. Is there any instruction on the hidden significance of forcefully interrupting the phase of the dissolution of sperm, egg, and wind energy?

The dissolution phases of appearance, increase, and attainment all relate exclusively to the phase of the dissolution of wind energy. Apparently, there are different explanations for the phases of dissolution relating to sperm, egg, and wind energy. In any case, those who attain enlightenment in this lifetime are far beyond the conventions of birth, death, and the bardo state. This is indicated by the way in which all the ordinary aggregates and elements—of which sperm, egg, and wind energy are most important—dissolve into the natural radiance of the sphere of clear light, the youthful vase body. For others, there is no bardo unless the aggregates and elements of this life, whether gross or subtle, dissolve entirely within the sphere of clear light. The visions of whiteness, redness, and blackness and so on are also signs of the dissolution of the subtle elements. We might indeed wonder then whether there is not a separate instruction. There is seemingly a variation in the degree to which the signs of dissolution are apparent based on differences in the individual.

7. Do the eight modes of arising and eight modes of dissolution occur for those liberated during the bardo of dying?

No, they do not. These modes of arising occur after the bardo of dying: they are modes of arising during the bardo of dharmatā and take place only after the earlier state has concluded.

8. Why is it said that in the bardo of dharmatā the peaceful forms do not act directly for the welfare of others, while the wrathful forms do?

This means that if we recognize the radiance of awareness when it arises as the peaceful forms from its base in our hearts, then, without any opportunity for acting directly to benefit others, they are absorbed directly into all-pervading space. Then, when the wrathful ones appear from the skull palace, they remain for several instants, acting for the welfare of others. Here, the "others" referred to in the phrase "acting for the welfare of others" does not signify separate beings to be trained, distinct from our own continuum. Rather, it means that these forms act on behalf of the dreamlike beings of the six classes who are spontaneously present, empty forms. This is explained in more detail in the section on the bardos in *The Treasury of the Supreme Vehicle*.

9. It is said that "directing awareness toward three thousand sentient beings causes them to be liberated." Does this refer to beings in the intermediate state or those in the natural bardo of this life? Would they all have previously trained in the Great Perfection? And is there any hidden significance to the figure of three thousand?

This question seems to be a reference to the following statement about the attainment of power over animation (of the two forms of power): "Directing pure awareness causes three thousand beings to be liberated."[1] Some say that sentient beings of the bardo can mean beings of the natural bardo of this life. Although it is not clear whether they are sentient beings who have trained previously in the Great Perfection, I think they must have some past connection. There appears to be no hidden significance to the figure of three thousand. Although such statements appear in the texts, we can only take them literally; we cannot explain the reason behind the numbers that are given—just as with statements about the bodhisattvas gaining twelve sets of one hundred qualities upon reaching the first bodhisattva stage, and so on.

10. Is it true that for those who are liberated in the bardo through the three crucial points, the eight modes of dissolution occur all at once, whereas for those who are deluded through lack of recognition, delusion continues because although the ground appearances could dissolve into inner space through the eight modes of dissolution, the habitual tendency for dissolution into saṃsāra is much stronger?

Dissolution can occur either through the strength of the liberation of the ground appearances or on the strength of delusion. Taking the second option, ordinary sentient beings will experience the arising of the ground appearances during the bardo of dharmatā for no longer than the duration of a shooting star. They will not recognize either their arising or their dissolution. Nevertheless, it is still true that through their habitual tendencies, the "arising as the impure saṃsāric gateway" has left the strongest impression, as a result of which saṃsāra continues to unfold with the bardos and with taking birth.

11. When there is fourfold wisdom, is there a disparity in enlightened qualities because liberation in the path experience of threefold wisdom does not perfect the strength of activity? Or is the strength of activity perfected in the path experience of the dissolution within the precious sphere of spontaneously present wisdom?

In fact, we must refer to an experience of *fourfold* wisdom (meaning the wisdom of dharmadhātu, mirrorlike wisdom, wisdom of equality, and wisdom of discernment), so it is slightly incorrect to refer to threefold wisdom. The perfection of the strength of all-accomplishing wisdom is said to occur only at the occasion of liberation into primordial purity. When this happens, the strength is already perfected, so it is meaningless to speak of this bringing about an emergence of greater or lesser qualities.

12. It is said that to accomplish the concentrations and formless absorptions we should meditate on the four-tiered A syllables and so on, but how is the meditation done?

The gaze should be as in *tögal* practice. Hold some gentle breathing for a while. Then, since A signifies the unborn, recognize that the unborn is the great all-pervading sphere of your own mind, and direct your gaze into space. There, visualize five red A syllables, one on top of another. And, by focusing your awareness undistractedly, allow it to transcend any referential focus, then settle evenly into that experience. The same applies for the remaining practices: the one with a stack of four white A syllables, and so on.

13. Is the hollow crystal light channel of wisdom the ultimate form of the central channel (avadhūti) in the Dzogchen tradition? Is it split in two as it extends to the two eyes?

I have the impression that it is just like that, but I recommend that you consult *The Treasury of the Supreme Vehicle*, as I cannot look at the text myself.

14. It is said that at death three drops of blood from the vital channel gather in the heart, causing a separation of mind and pure awareness, after which awareness departs through the eyes. Is this referring to the coarse visual faculty?

This refers not to the coarse faculty support but to the light channel—the far-reaching lasso of water lamp—which is connected to the eyes. It is this interdependent circumstance that allows the visions of the bardo of dharmatā to arise.

15. In the pith instructions of the Ancient Translations, it is said that the right channel (rasana) is white and the left channel (lalanā) is red. Can we say that the right is the potential for the grasped (or perceived) and the left is the potential for the grasper (or perceiver)?

Yes, I think that would be fine.

16. What is the significance of the explanation in the bardo aspiration prayer of the Heart Essence of the Vast Expanse that the experience of redness arises before the experience of whiteness?

It does indeed appear as if the sequence of the three symbolic experiences as redness, whiteness, and blackness is the vision of *The Aspiration Prayer for Purifying the Realms of the Three Kāyas*. Still, in other works, such as the bardo aspiration prayer *Ocean of Single Intent, Yogic Exercises of the Awareness Holders Involving Channels and Wind Energies*, and the earlier and later sections of *The Chariot to Omniscience*, the omniscient Jigme Lingpa describes the usual sequence of whiteness, redness, and blackness. I wonder, therefore, whether we can be certain that the earlier text is not corrupted by scribal error.

17. In the method for bringing the chains of awareness within the enclosure of the lamp of empty spheres, are there any other instructions besides training with diligence and applying the three crucial points, the gazes and so on, having gained stability in trekchö, so that awareness is not disrupted by wind energy and mind?

The most crucial point for meditation is to gradually bring the chains of awareness that arise outside the empty lamps into the center of those empty lamps by means of the gaze, and then not to allow that awareness to stray elsewhere but to plant it like a spear. As a support for this, you also need to apply the crucial points of body and speech, and so on.

18. Is what we call genuine or ordinary consciousness the nature of the mind, the self-arising primordial wisdom that is untainted by thoughts associated with the past, present, and future? In any case, what is meant by "ordinary" and "consciousness" here?

The term *genuine mind* refers to exactly what you have written. Yet, as this is the most important point among all the ocean-like statements in Highest Yoga Tantra, it is, like the ocean itself, decidedly vast and profound. Terms such as *vajra of the mind, clear light,* and *natural and coemergent* are more common in the Highest Yoga class, while *ordinary consciousness* appears to be particularly prevalent in Dzogchen.

The section on general conduct in the *Moonlight* commentary[2] on medicine states that the force of a yawn, a sneeze, and so on, should not be blocked, and that to remain ordinary, in this way, prevents ill health. The text uses the expression "remain ordinary" in the sense of remaining naturally. In a similar way, the word *ordinary* can refer to the genuine state, left naturally as it is, without any contrivance or adjustment through abandoning or adopting, elimination or cultivation. The reason the term is used so frequently in a Dzogchen context is that this differs from other means of bringing about the dawn of wisdom. Other perfection-stage systems employ various methods to generate a feeling of bliss or an experience of nonconceptuality, such as focusing the mind on the channels, wind energies, and drops. But here, by contrast, the introduction and meditation are effected directly upon our everyday state of conceptualization, by leaving the mind as it is, in a state of naked, all-penetrating awareness, primordially free and beyond any notion of anything to be eliminated or preserved. This is also the key to why this approach is praised so extensively as the effortless vehicle. The sense of *consciousness* here is that the essence of awareness is unlike inanimate matter or some lifeless vacuity, insofar as it has a quality of cognizance or awareness. This is easy to understand.

19. When we sustain the nonconceptual practice of the union of awareness and emptiness, any rising thoughts are freed upon arising, impartially. And yet, with all three modes of liberation, distraction can still occur, undetected, through our innumerable extremely subtle "undercurrent" thoughts. Can we put a stop to this diffuse form of delusive thought through continual reliance upon the flow of natural, self-arisen mindfulness as we abide in an experience of the natural state?

Even though we might settle evenly in what we take to be a state of awareness, at some point we will be deceived by the indeterminate ground-of-all. When this happens, we will find ourselves in a stagnant state of mental stillness, a blankness or oblivion, in which we do not notice the undercurrent of thoughts. At this stage, meditative equipoise is not yet secure, so no matter how familiar we are with the practice, we are unable to counteract the habitual tendencies of delusive thought. Rather than trying to control all the various good and bad thoughts as they arise, we should hold to the very essence of unimpeded awareness, which is the basis of such arising. We must sharpen and intensify this quality of awareness, again and again. By laying bare this awareness and sustaining it and it alone, we will not be tempted to evaluate any subtle or coarse thoughts that may arise. This does not mean that we are distracted and fail to notice what arises, but that we are no longer captivated by or distracted by expressive thoughts. This corresponds to the third mode of liberation, which is compared to a thief entering an empty house. The more familiar we become with this experience, the more the expressive power or strength of ordinary conceptual thoughts will be cut through and the strength of nonconceptual awareness perfected. And with this, as it is said, the spear of awareness will circle within the sphere of emptiness. Actual self-arising, natural mindfulness is nothing other than the capacity for remembrance that is a timeless quality of genuine mind itself. It should be clear from what has just been said that the mindfulness that maintains a boundary between distraction and nondistraction while remaining in the expressive power of awareness is merely an approximation of true, natural mindfulness.

20. Are cognitive experiences the same as "complete experiences"? Is the distinction between visionary and cognitive experiences a matter of whether there is stability? If so, then if the empty forms described in other Highest Yoga tantras were stable, how would they differ from the visionary experiences spoken of in Dzogchen?

When we speak of the three types of experience—cognitive, visionary, and complete—the first refers to experiences of bliss, clarity, and absence of thought and so on. The second type includes the lamp of absolute space, which is compared to the fan of a peacock's feathers, and the lamp of empty spheres, which are like the rippling circles from a stone cast into a pond. The third type includes experiences that are signs of wind energy, such as those compared to the sun, the moon, and a rainbow, which appear to be distinct from the radiance of awareness. Therefore, we cannot claim that these various experiences are the same.

The empty forms described in other classes of Tantra are like the visionary experiences of the Dzogchen practice of tögal only in the sense that both are empty forms. It is true, however, that they are also similar in that both grow progressively clearer and more stable with increased familiarity. But, as *The Treasury of the Supreme Vehicle* explains, there is a great difference in their aspects of brightness or their aspects of clarity and stability. While one is a manifestation of wind energy, the other is a manifestation of awareness. Molasses, milk, and sugarcane are similar in having a sweet taste, but there is still a great difference among them. And although we can experience this difference with our tongue, even

Sarasvatī herself is unable to express it in words, as the master Daṇḍin observed.

21. There is a union of clarity and emptiness in the ordinary mind, and there are meditative experiences of bliss, clarity, and absence of thought, which derive from this union. Then there is the union of clarity and emptiness in the pure awareness beyond mind, together with its bliss, clarity, and absence of thought. Can we say that the difference between these two sets is a difference between the Pith Instruction category of the Great Perfection and what lies below it?

The union of clarity and emptiness in the ordinary mind, and the bliss, clarity, and absence of thought that are its qualities, cannot be classified above even the calm abiding that is common to both non-Buddhist outsiders and Buddhist insiders. Any of the three Dzogchen categories, whether Mind, Expanse, or Pith Instructions, is generally more profound than even the perfection phase of Highest Yoga Tantra, which in turn belongs to the Secret Mantra that is superior to the general Mahāyāna. I think that to make such an assertion is therefore inappropriate.

22. When dividing the Great Perfection into three categories, can we relate the Mind category to Mahāyoga, the Expanse category to Anuyoga, and the Pith Instruction category to Atiyoga?

I do not see anything too inappropriate about such a proposition. It even resembles what the *Dispelling the Darkness of the Ten Directions* commentary says about how the gradual path of the *Illusory Secret Essence* and the Dzogchen practices of trekchö and tögal relate to the three of Ati, Mahā, and so on.[3] Still, the matter requires further investigation.

23. Is it correct to say that when yogis who meditate on the Great Perfection are liberated in any of the three earlier bardos, they awaken at that very moment in the primordial sphere; whereas if they are liberated in the bardo of becoming, they are reborn in a natural nirmāṇakāya pure realm and awakened there?

Yes, it is just as you have written.

24. When speaking of the indivisibility of the two higher truths, can we say that the relative is embraced by a special motivation and conduct of the indivisible two truths, so that we view everything as the pure maṇḍala of the vajra sphere, while recognizing that the seven riches of the absolute are always spontaneously present?[4] And that the indivisibility of these two truths, which are greater than the two common forms of equality, is great dharmakāya?[5]

It is indeed so. Still, you must understand higher relative truth in more detail from the explanations of how appearances are established as divine. Although the fundamental point of the seven riches of the absolute depends on fully ascertaining the genuine nature of mind, it is also worth consulting the tantra commentaries. Yet for fear that this might become too verbose, I shall not elaborate further here.

This concludes my rough answers to your questions.

These days, we have reached the end of a degenerate age, in which the teachings of Buddha are on the wane and people have little faith in the sacred Dharma. The teaching and practice of the supreme vehicle, the vajra pinnacle, are barely alive, and what remains is due to merit and fortune. At such a time, knowing that even finding the opportunity for discussion is a sign of good fortune, I am like a mere child imitating an adult. For how could I ever explain such profound vajra topics? To judge from your questions, you are studying and contemplating the Heart Essence of the Great Perfection a great deal—in this, I greatly and sincerely rejoice.

The following topics are clearly and incisively resolved in *The Treasury of Scriptural Authority*, the commentary to *The Treasury of the Dharmadhātu*, which is just like the omniscient king of Dharma, Drime Özer, in person:

- the general understanding of the distinction between mind and pure awareness
- the means of directly recognizing pure awareness
- how this alone eliminates all the potential dangers of sidetracks, pitfalls, and errors
- how to pursue pure awareness alone, without spoiling it through superfluous instructions
- how all the crucial points of the path taught in the sūtras and lower tantras are included within this approach, and not only that, but also how it is unlike any lower vehicle and superior to them

You should therefore consult the text repeatedly. If you read it again and again, your understanding will grow in precision and certainty, and you will develop an insatiable, heartfelt wish to study further. But consulting it only once or twice will not take you beyond a vague, superficial understanding.

The Treasury of the Supreme Vehicle brings about a vast, decisive understanding of both trekchö and tögal, so it is vital that you study that too. I also believe that the *Great Chariot* commentary to *Finding Comfort and Ease in the Nature of Mind* and the root text and commentaries of the *Treasury of Precious Qualities*[6] are extremely important, as they are indispensable for gaining an understanding of the general structure of the teachings.

I respectfully submit this direct and familiar, if perhaps inelegant, response.

This was offered by the old beggar Tenpe Nyima, the lowest servant of the Jamyang Guru, the great Vajradhara. May virtue abound!

10

PLEASE DEBATE THE MESSENGER

The kingdom of Derge was the epicenter of the nonsectarian movement, and, in the words of E. Gene Smith, "the intellectual and artistic heart of eastern Tibet." Many of the most prominent teachers associated with the movement lived within the kingdom's borders, and its capital, Derge Gönchen—taking its name from the great Sakya monastery (*gönchen*) of Lhundrup Teng—was where many of the works most readily associated with the movement were edited and produced. Of the various projects undertaken at the great "Dharma Treasury" printing house, renowned for its authoritative editions of the Buddhist canon, none was more controversial than the publication of the collected writings of the Sakya scholar Gorampa Sönam Senge (1429–1489). Printing took place in the early years of the twentieth century as the culmination of an arduous process of compilation and editing. In one account, the project was initially conceived in response to a question. Khenpo Jamyang Chökyi Gyaltsen (1870–1940) asked his teacher, Khenpo Shenpen Nangwa, what could be done to reverse the decline in the Sakya school's fortunes. Shenpen Nangwa deliberated for several days before suggesting the publication of Gorampa's writings. Like many other controversial texts at odds with mainstream Geluk thought, these works had effectively been banned in central Tibet for more than a century. And, with restrictions on even the copying of manuscripts, study of the texts had seriously declined.

Jamyang Chökyi Gyaltsen devoted several years to the project of gathering and editing copies of the texts. Some say he spent years traveling through Tibet in search of manuscripts. One account even tells how he came close to losing them all when his mule was nearly swept away in a river. Ultimately, however, the printing was a success. With the assistance of Jamyang Khyentse Chökyi Lodrö and others, the books were distributed throughout Eastern Tibet so that they could be taught in monastic colleges. And similar projects, focused on other major Sakya works, soon followed.

But the revival of Sakya learning stoked anti-Gelukpa sentiment in the Derge region—at least that was the feeling of Amdo Geshe Jampal Rolwe Lodrö (1888–1936). In the letter translated below, which likely dates from the mid-1920s, Jampal Rolwe Lodrö notes the popularity of Gorampa's works, as well as those of other leading Sakya philosophers, Shākya Chokden (1428–1507) and Taktsang Lotsāwa Sherab Rinchen (b.1405). He claims that many monks took such polemical works—as he calls them—to be definitive, leading them to refute "the precious doctrine of the noble Dharma king, the great Tsongkhapa." He therefore challenges anyone holding such views to a debate. But this is not before he demonstrates his own nonsectarian values by praising every major Tibetan school and identifying himself as a true follower of all their highest teachings.

Jampal Rolwe Lodrö was certainly ecumenical. Following his monastic education in the great Geluk monastery of Kumbum Jampa Ling in Amdo, he went on to study with, among others, Jamyang Khyentse Wangpo, the "crazy yogi" and Longchen Nyingtik lineage holder Khamnyön Dharma Senge, and Tertön Sogyal Lerab Lingpa. And just like his root teacher, the famous Gelukpa scholar Drakkar Tulku Lobzang Palden Tendzin Nyendrak (1866–1928), he took a special interest in, and wrote about, the Great Perfection. In addition to his thirteen-chapter treatise on Dzogchen entitled *The Heart Essence of the Great Perfection of Mañjuśrī*, he also wrote a series of verses praising Longchen Rabjam.[1]

It is unclear whether anyone responded to Jampal Rolwe Lodrö's call for a debate. In later years, his appeals against sectarianism were renewed by his foremost disciple, Dongak Chökyi Gyatso (as seen in chapter 12). And even though the writings of Gorampa were widely taught, they remained divisive: even as late as 1940, the controversial Gelukpa teacher Pabongkhapa Dechen Nyingpo

(1878–1941) criticized Gorampa's "wicked compositions and faulty statements," noting scornfully that reading transmissions and teachings were granted although the lineage had been broken. But such remarks represent another strand of the Geluk school, an exclusivism that contrasts sharply with what Amdo Geshe wrote— in what was an *open* letter in more ways than one.

The Messenger of
Authentic Reasoning

A Letter Initiating the Occasion for Debate Sent from
Derge Lhundrup Teng, a Great Center of the Two Traditions,
to the Scholars of the Region

AMDO GESHE JAMPAL ROLWE LODRÖ

Like the brilliant sun, you thoroughly illuminate the Sage's
teachings,
Splendid wisdom of the victorious buddhas of past, present, and
future, together with their heirs;
O Mañjuśrī guru, you who reveal the path in its entirety,
Grant me the auspiciousness of showering down a rain of
virtuous signs!

The perfect Buddha independently revealed the excellent path of
profound interdependence that is without delusion;
Sacred Dharma, profound and vast—the supreme vehicle's
truths of cessation and path—protects us from existence and
quiescence;
And the saṅgha of the noble assembly, companions in
accomplishment, has all the qualities of knowledge and
liberation.
In these three authentic sources of refuge, beyond deception,
I take refuge until attaining great awakening!

Embellishing the universally luminous space of the Buddha's
teachings
With myriad, weblike rays of the light of scripture and reasoning,

You are the sun and moon in the lineage of the profound and vast
   gradual path.
To this line of successive teachers I bow down in homage!

Thoroughly intoxicated with realization, having insatiably imbibed
The essential nectar of the Ancient Translations' three classes and
   nine spaces,
You never tire of upholding the precious supreme vehicle.
May you, foremost among the learned and accomplished, be
   victorious!

Every aspect of the five sciences is perfectly complete
In this, the divine path of realizing the absence of constructs,
The Sakya tradition with its light of well-spoken nectar.
May it remain as an ornament for the locks of Śambhu!

Marpa's ultimate intent, the genuine face of reality,
The unaltered natural state is the meaning of Mahāmudrā;
This great path of the lineage of wholly accomplished siddhas
I praise as the very route the buddhas of the three times take.

Within the nature of uncommon bliss and emptiness,
Karma and *kleśas* are transformed through the alchemy of
   realizing the nature of emptiness.
May this vajra yoga, in which the actual Kālacakra of union is
   brought about directly,
Reign supreme!

Gathering all the finest parts, with nothing omitted,
The scalpel of the well said clears the mind's eye in immature
   disciples;
Distilling the essence of an ocean of sūtras and tantras, from
   kārikas to *Guhyasamāja*,[2]
The well said, arranged in jewel garlands, can adorn all those
   whose intelligence is clear.

Blazing in splendor to dispel the darkness of confusion
And uproot the malady of sectarian prejudice,
These fine explanations are like the king of wish-granting jewels,
The sweet fame of the noble-minded Lobzang Drakpa,[3] skilled in
    bringing a gentle rain of light.

He wears a diadem upon his locks and has a single eye in his
    forehead,
The quintessence of the Buddha's teaching is like his heart.
Upon the ground of righteous impartiality is the mountain of
    intellect,
And at its peak, upon snowy mounds of scripture and reasoning,
Are the descendants of this learned and physically strong five-faced
    lord, the king of lions,[4]
Who towers above others, bears a turquoise mane of analysis based
    on the four modes of applied reasoning,
And subdues the foxes of wrong view through the clear roar of
    realizing the point of meditation.
Who would dare to dance and play upon the sharp claws of scripture
    and reasoning?

Untainted by the mental stains of the eight vehicles
And beyond all the speculations of lesser realization and rituals,
I have realized the very face of the spontaneously present three kāyas,
The ultimate destination of all paths of sūtra and mantra.

Let the immature who have pledged themselves
To the tradition of the Omniscient One,
The tantras of the Ancient Translations and vision of Padmākara
    and Vimalamitra,
Take care to avoid vague settling, vacant emptiness, or ordinary
    mental clarity!

If there are some who disagree with most scholars,
Whose minds are impartial and intellects powerful,

Let them not whisper and gossip away in secret
But come here and debate directly in my presence!

All that is done with attachment and aversion brings ruin upon
    ourselves and others.
The single gateway to peaceful and impartial engagement
Appears through knowledge of the authentic word and treatises.
Who dares cross the bounds of reason that the pioneering
    scholars have set?

The real meaning of the three collections[5] and four classes of
    Tantra[6]
Is complete within the tradition of the three visions[7] and three
    continua.[8]
I take as my thesis the indivisibility of saṃsāra and nirvāṇa,
In which all knowable things are clear and there is no clinging to
    extremes even in name.

Without relying on an understanding of sūtra or mantra,
Saying "not clinging to anything, neither existence nor
    nonexistence,"
And directly contradicting the glorious Sakya tradition—
Be careful, you who presume to call yourselves Sakyapa!

Not accepting that phenomena are empty of their own essence
And have their own unique characteristics,
While denying direct perception—such a system of thought
Is worse than even the Cārvāka, so how could it be Buddhist?[9]

That the maṇḍala of the genuine, coemergent nature represents
    eternalism,
And the absence of true nature in the Muni's realization
    represents nihilism—
To persist in such assertions while claiming to follow
    Candrakīrti's tradition

Is like shamelessly running about unclothed: a source of hilarity
  for others!

Entities are obstructing; what is permanent can produce an
  effect;
And an effect can be present in a cause: examine such claims,
Which you hold to be the assertions of the omniscient Sakyapa,
And weigh them against the excellent sayings of the Five
  Patriarchs![10]

The genuine nature that is freed from the cocoon of confusion,
Through the guru's instruction and outer and inner
  skill-in-means,
Which all those who are learned and accomplished know to be
The essence of clear light Mahāmudrā—this I accept.

While unclear as to what distinguishes contrived and
  uncontrived,
To assert that all knowing and perception is fabricated,
And shamelessly claim that remaining in a dull state of mind
Is the Kagyü way—take care to avoid such statements!

Core advice on the meaning of the Father and Mother tantras,
Distinguishing views that bring mental activity to cessation—
This, I know, is complete herein, and therefore
All those with critical intelligence, please explain at length!

In mind's actual condition, karma and kleśas are indeed
  "other-empty,"
And this is not the same as one thing being empty of itself:
Such is my assertion, based on both the intent and literal message
Of the sūtras teaching the buddha nature.

Not simply repeating the earlier sayings of Sakya and Geluk,
Some invalidate what is lower with higher forms of reasoning.

If so, let it not develop further and lead to harsh words
But extend the chain of scripture and reasoning, a cause of joy!

Transgressing the boundaries set by the founders of tradition
And spurred on by confidently propounding nonsense,
To support your own position while refuting the positions of
    others,
Without even the slightest mastery of the signs of negation or
    proof,
And failing to rely upon the logical works of the Six
    Ornaments—
Even while not claiming that this represents a lineage tradition,
To explain the scriptures while thinking that you are
Following the great pioneers is something to be celebrated.
And yet, without realizing the natural state of your own mind,
Even if you were to offer a great many independent explanations,
The learned must investigate and examine them
Asking how they relate to the two major philosophical
    traditions.[11]

The ultimate Secret Mantra path, the Great Perfection,
The essence of Highest Yoga Tantra, Mahāmudrā,
The indivisibility of saṃsāra and nirvāṇa, the path of clarity and
    emptiness without grasping,[12]
And the profound path of Vajra Yoga—these ultimate practices
Are the union of the Profound View and great secret Vajrayāna.
This is the fundamental point of the teachings in Jamgön
    Tsongkhapa's lineage,
Bliss and emptiness indivisible, a single taste in essence—
This is my thesis, indelibly inscribed.

Those at the summit of learning who wish to dispute this
Should exercise caution, just as ordinary snow lions,
Even as they shake their thick manes of merit,
Take care to avoid the teeth and claws of eight-legged Śarabha.

Even if I do not explain in a biased way, saying this is not
The meaning of the scriptural tradition accepted by the wise,
My stable thesis is that this does not accord with the
    fundamental point
Of the three major commentaries of glorious Candrakīrti.[13]

In the ocean of Tantra, sealed with the six limits and four
    modes,[14]
The churning stick of infinite instructions on theory and practice
Produces the essence, the sun of what is well spoken,
Renowned as an adornment in the sky of Buddha's teachings.

Nevertheless, the fresh winds of sophistry
Bring a cloud canopy to the scriptural tradition,
And for the childish clambering upon the platform of concealing
    words,
Actual liberation appears like an illusion.

Just as the illusory lion and illusory elephant
May become illusory brothers,
I take delight in the illusory creation of these few echoes.
Let all who seek illusory liberation look here!

I offer the following message, ushered in with these verses, to the
great beings who uphold the teachings in this great region.

It is renowned and well established here, in the Land of Snow
Mountains, that all the precious teachings of the victorious Buddha are not contradictory. I myself have had the good fortune to
receive the sustenance of ripening and liberating instructions of
the Ancient and New schools of Secret Mantra from several noble
instructors, who practice according to the Dharma. As it says in
"Praise of One More Eminent Than the Gods":

I do not cling to Buddha's position,
Nor do I despise Kapila and the rest.

I simply accept whatever is revealed
By one who speaks words of reason.[15]

As this indicates, we must apply our minds sincerely to a thorough examination of the three domains of evaluation, using the three forms of valid cognition related to direct perception and inference. The outcome of such investigation will be that, without slipping into sectarian bias or prejudice, we will realize how all forms of Buddhist teaching are equally effective as means of attaining omniscience. Moreover, any difference in terminology between earlier and later traditions of explanation will be seen simply as reflecting variations in practice, while ultimately pointing toward the same destination. Inspired by this kind of confidence, we will feel great reverence for all authentic holders of the teachings and their excellent explanations.

These days, there are many who cause sectarian division in the precious teachings of the Victorious One, and many who refute the precious teachings of the noble Dharma king, the great Tsongkhapa, in particular. As a result, students who rely on me for teachings, both permanent residents and occasional visitors to this place, have persistently pleaded with me, burning my ears by saying:

> Nowadays the precious teachings of the Victorious One are at a low ebb, without the slightest trace of true exposition, debate, or composition. In particular, people take as definitive the comments in the polemical texts of Gorampa, Shākya Chokden, and Taktsang Lotsāwa, which assert that the scriptural works of Tsongkhapa, the Dharma king of the three realms, are entirely at fault. The scholars of this region declare that there has not been the slightest response on the subject of the Secret Mantra, while earlier and later replies to objections on the sūtras merely listed one or two faults, without really proving meaningful. Thus, you must answer them.

In response, I hereby dispatch this letter inviting debate, in the manner described in the sacred Dharma of the Vinaya. Through this, may any honest scholars who wish to repair the teachings make themselves known to me whenever there is any conflict and a desire to refute the excellent explanations of the great Jamgön, the king of Dharma, Tsongkhapa. Jampal Rolwe Lodrö sends this in all directions. May it prove auspicious!

11

Demolition, Dzogchen Style

How much knowledge of Buddhist philosophy is required for the practice of the Great Perfection? Must a practitioner be familiar with Nāgārjuna's Middle Way, for example? Or does it suffice to be introduced to the nature of mind by a qualified guru? Mipham famously equated the view of trekchö with the view of the Middle Way, writing that "both glorious Candrakīrti in the noble land of India and Rongzom Chökyi Zangpo in Tibet proclaimed the great emptiness of primordial purity, at one in their intention and with a single voice."[1] Yet, as is clear from "A Lamp to Dispel Darkness" (see chapter 4), he also believed that village yogis, or those with little or no formal education, could still practice Dzogchen meditation successfully. Other writers have also discussed this topic. For Dodrupchen Jigme Tenpe Nyima, for example, the pointing out of pure awareness, which marks the real beginning of the Dzogchen path, can come only after an introduction to emptiness:

> Even without the claim that awareness and emptiness
> Are like the ends of a balance moving up and down,
> If a disciple's stage of realization is considered,
> It is only after emptiness has been introduced
> That pure awareness is pointed out, say those who know the
> profound.[2]

Indeed, this view reflects the standard presentation of the Dzogchen path, which begins with preliminary practices intended to "destroy the house of the ordinary mind" before proceeding to the introduction to pure awareness and the main practice. The preliminaries are said to be essential. And this means that even exceptional individuals of the very highest capacity, who can leap directly to the main practice, must have gone through the preliminaries at some point in a previous existence.

Instructions on the preliminaries vary from one lineage to the next, but the most common form in the Heart Essence (Nyingtik) tradition as it is practiced today includes three sections: (1) probing to the root of the mind, (2) searching for mind's hidden flaws, and (3) investigating mind's coming, staying, and going. Jamyang Khyentse Chökyi Lodrö explains the first two as follows:

> *Probing to the root of mind* means investigating which of the three doors (of body, speech, and mind) it is that causes us to wander throughout beginningless time in saṃsāra and which it is that carries out virtuous or unvirtuous actions. When investigating, we discover mind to be the most important factor. *Searching for hidden flaws* means examining whether body, speech, and mind are unitary or distinct and finding that, while on a conventional level they appear to be related, ultimately there is no real entity called "mind" that could be one with, or distinct from, anything else.[3]

The third section, involving the investigation of mind's coming, staying, and going, is even more prevalent than the first two (it is explained in detail, for example, in Jigme Lingpa's *Yeshe Lama*) Jamyang Khyentse Chökyi Lodrö summarizes its conclusions in the following way:

> When you investigate the essence of this mind, even if you search for its arising you cannot find it. There is no reality to the mind's apparent presence. Nor is there anywhere that it ceases. It is thus without foundation or origin.

All texts emphasize that it is not enough simply to know intellectually and superficially that the mind is without foundation or origin; we must develop certainty in this conclusion. And such conviction can come only from extended personal reflection and contemplation. Yukhok Chatralwa mentions a tradition of focusing on the investigation of coming, staying, and going for a period of three years. And there are stories of Patrul Rinpoche encouraging disciples to go out into the hills and forests and to search for the mind everywhere, even under rocks and leaves, as if in a literal interpretation of the instruction to leave no stone unturned.

In the following text, Yukhok Chatralwa expresses his disapproval of any version of the preliminary investigations that lacks thoroughness or precision.[4] For him, this clearly means failing to apply Mipham's unique Nyingma perspective on selflessness and emptiness. Above all, it would be inappropriate, he warns, to mix non-Nyingma ideas with what is, after all, a particularly Nyingma practice.

This concern to represent the views of Mipham even leads Yukhok Chatralwa to take a seemingly different approach to Nyoshul Lungtok Tenpe Nyima, Patrul Rinpoche's foremost heir in the Dzogchen lineage. The variance concerns whether there should be any subtle viewpoint during the preliminaries (a topic addressed at some length in Mipham's *Beacon of Certainty*).[5] Mipham believes some subtle viewpoint is necessary in the beginning, in order, for example, to understand selflessness. Nevertheless, once the truth has been seen directly, there is no need in the subsequent certainty to continue holding on to selflessness as a point of view. The same applies to emptiness. As Mipham puts it, the ultimate is "seen" only in an experience of nonseeing; it is not a matter of holding an object in mind. Or, as Tertön Sogyal is quoted as saying in the text below, maintaining a viewpoint would make the Dzogchen preliminaries as much of an exercise in building up the house of the ordinary mind as one of tearing it apart.

Although Yukhok Chatralwa refers to Mipham and Dodrupchen Jigme Tenpe Nyima in this text and elsewhere in his writings too, he did not meet either master directly. He once had an opportunity to see Mipham, it is said, but his teacher, Adzom Drukpa (1842–1924), would not grant him permission to leave their encampment and make the journey. Later, however, he met Mipham many times in visions. And he often taught from Mipham's works, especially *The Beacon of Certainty*, *The Essence of Clear Light* overview of the *Guhyagarbha Tantra*, and the *Trilogy on the Genuine Nature of Mind*, claiming that they hold the key to understanding the writings of Longchen Rabjam.

Although Yukhok Chatralwa never met Jigme Tenpe Nyima in person either, he still considered him his teacher, on account of all that he received from him indirectly through Tertön Sogyal as an intermediary. On the one occasion when the two came closest to meeting, Jigme Tenpe Nyima's health deteriorated, and a frustrated Yukhok Chatralwa was left to lament, "The merit of Tibet is weak. How lowly is the fortune of the Nyingma school! My own karma too must be especially feeble!"[6]

Those of us who didn't have the good fortune, merit, or karma to meet Yukhok Chatralwa in person still have a chance to study with him indirectly through his writings too. And even now more of these texts continue to be discovered, edited, and published. What follows is but a single jewel from the treasure trove that is his collected writings on the Great Perfection.

How to Practice the Path of the Great Perfection

Yukhok Chatralwa Chöying Rangdrol

Generally, there are three parts to practicing the path of the clear light Great Perfection: preliminaries, main part, and conclusion.

The preliminary, which is the instruction on demolishing the house of the ordinary mind, itself includes three sections: (1) probing to the root, (2) searching for hidden flaws, and (3) investigating coming, staying, and going.

Probing to the Root

In this instruction, which is likened to identifying a thief, we must recognize the source of our circling in saṃsāra. This is the point at which most teachers these days tell their students, "Analyze your body, speech, and mind. Determine which is most important." The students then contemplate all manner of chatter and hearsay before concluding that mind is most important because it is the one that originally became deluded, and so on. Then the teacher will say such things as "Investigate whether your mind has features such as color or shape. Analyze its coming, staying, and going." Then when the students say, "There is nothing to it at all," the teacher will say they have understood. Then the teacher will continue: "Now settle the mind without altering. . . . Now direct your awareness . . . and so on."[7] Yet for such explanations, it would hardly be necessary to shut the outer door from the outside, lock the inner door from the inside, or apply the seal of strictest secrecy! For this does not correspond to any tradition of Mahāmudrā, Great Perfection, or the Middle Way. And as it is perfectly intelligible even to an old nun, there would have been no need for Vajradhara to appear in order to reveal it. We must bring an end to such terrible traditions from now on.

In our own tradition, we assert that it is clinging to the self of the individual that is at the root of saṃsāra. By this, we mean a mistaken mind that perceives a self or an "I" in the five psychophysical aggregates, or the body, speech, and mind. This is what brings clinging to an "I" or a self, and therefore we say that it is certainly how the object of refutation appears. Clinging to an individual self, then, is the root of saṃsāra, whereas clinging to a phenomenal self (or identity) is considered a cognitive obscuration. For, as the regent Maitreya states:

> Any thought involving the three spheres
> Is a cognitive obscuration, it is claimed.[8]

This assertion applies both in the sūtras and in mantra. And there is no need to transform it into something else, to patch it up with something else, or to mix it with something else. Syncretism, in other words, is inappropriate. Why so? Adherents of the later tradition apply the term *truly existent* to the object of negation and claim that this is certainly what is to be negated. They believe that clinging to things as truly existent is an emotional obscuration, and they therefore contend that it is clinging to phenomenal identity that lies at the root of saṃsāra. And since it is rather uncomfortable for a single person to hold in the mind two contradictory beliefs concerning the root of saṃsāra at the same time, such syncretism is out of place.

Moreover, in our own tradition we make further assertions, such as that the śrāvakas and pratyekabuddhas do not realize the selflessness of phenomena completely, while others claim that they do. It would not be right, therefore, to combine these two systems. Of course, it is fine to mix two things that complement each other and go together well, like wild sweet potato and melted butter, but there is no need to mix things that do not. In our tradition, for example, it is important to develop a deep certainty from within and to resolve things decisively. In other traditions, it is important to maintain faith and pure perception until reaching the essence of enlightenment, so they are known as systems for honorable beings. Generally, there are said to be more than six[9] major philosophical systems here in Tibet, each with its own complete path to liberation and enlightenment, and therefore there is no need to combine them.

SEARCHING FOR HIDDEN FLAWS

You might wonder how self-clinging functions. It involves clinging to the self as something whole, singular, and real. When it comes to overturning such clinging, the antidote to singularity is multiplicity. Breaking down the self into five aggregates and then (to take form alone) to the level of the partless particle thus counteracts the notion of the self as singular. As the antidote to the idea that the self is real, we can consider how it is false and impermanent, meaning that it has the character of changing with each passing moment. This corresponds to the subtle impermanence of its nature. The self is also impermanent at the coarser level of its continuum. It is therefore merely the interdependent connection of causes and conditions, and there is nothing more to it than this—no true existence. When we realize this, it naturally dispels any clinging to self, so this is the realization of individual selflessness.

At the stage of analyzing whether body, speech, or mind is most important, the assertion is that mind is the most important factor.[10] Still, when you examine the matter closely, you find that the body is also of great significance. For instance, when entering the door of the Buddhist teachings, there can be no entrance other than by means of the prātimokṣa, bodhisattva, and mantra precepts. And for the prātimokṣa vows to arise initially in your continuum you must be either a man or a woman and not just from any of the three continents, but specifically someone with the special physical support that is unique to this continent of Jambudvīpa. The vows will not arise in anyone else, not in devas, nāgas, garuḍas, or any other such being. And even if the Buddha were to appear in person before these other beings, even he could not help to change this. And even though the bodhisattva vows can arise in such beings as devas, nāgas, and the like, they do not come about through mind alone; they require the combination of body, speech, and mind. In entering the door of Unsurpassed Mantra, only the physical support of a human form complete with its six elements is suitable as a vessel for the four empowerments, because without it there is no associated cause. Similarly, even if all eighteen freedoms and advantages are complete, the body is most important. For example, a newborn baby without sight or hearing will be incapable of learning even the slightest dharmic or worldly action. The body is therefore of great importance.

In a similar way, speech too is said to be very important. Revealing what must be avoided or adopted, for example, requires all the qualities of speech, as you must be able to speak and understand. Merely making sounds like an animal is of no benefit. Communication involves the body, speech, and mind. It is by means of the chest, throat, tongue, teeth, palate, and so on, as well as through mental motivation, that all words and their corresponding meanings are produced, in dependence on the garlands of syllables, the speech that rides on the horse of wind energy. Speech too is therefore of great importance.

Without the mind, which includes the eight collections of consciousness and fifty accompanying mental states, we would be no more than a corpse. It is mind that first arises in saṃsāra. Body and speech are continually acquired and left behind.

Self-clinging appears through the force of ignorance and delusion. It is through attachment to how things appear, and through solidifying that attachment and clinging to it as real, that we cling to a self and what belongs to that self—in other words, "I" and "mine." This is how, like a herdsman with his herd, we cling to what we take to be ours, or what we imagine belongs to the self.

Generally, there is no beginning to saṃsāra, no beginning to birth, and no beginning to delusion. We wander in saṃsāric existence, therefore, until we put an end to it. And throughout this time spent in the impure realms of saṃsāra, the individual wanderer does not have a mind in isolation but the three factors of body, speech, and mind together. The realms we wander through are of six types—the abodes of the six classes of beings in saṃsāra. Correspondingly, therefore, there are various types of body. The body of the desire realms is material and made of flesh and blood. In the form realms, there is a subtle body of light. And in the formless realms, beings have a mental "meditation" body. From the Mahāyāna viewpoint, we accumulate karma based on body, speech, and mind. And it is only through accumulating karma that we are reborn in the three realms of saṃsāra. It would be impossible for the mind alone, without accumulating karma, to be reborn in saṃsāra. There is no such thing as a solitary mind, with no accumulated karma, being pulled along like a fish caught on a hook, or pursued like deer chased by dogs. It is through karma alone that rebirth takes place. As it is said, "The world is created through karma; it is through karma that it appears. Karma is what creates it all, like an artist." Tainted karma is of three kinds: virtuous, unvirtuous, and unalterable. Yet whichever of these is accumulated, it is based on body, speech, and mind together. The mind cannot function in isolation.

It is also impossible for there to be only enlightened mind—rather than enlightened body, speech, and mind together—in a pure buddha realm. Body, speech, and mind work in combination, therefore, like the legs of a tripod. And it is difficult to identify which of them is most important. Nevertheless, from sūtra to mantra, it is said that mind is the most important. So, having been introduced to this analysis, you must investigate and analyze the matter for yourself. But anything other than deep certainty, based on an understanding that does not contradict scripture, reasoning, or the pith instructions, is not entirely pure.

COMING, STAYING, AND GOING

There are many traditions of explanation from the lineage of past vidyādhara masters, such as *Settling into Natural Rest Through Trekchö*[11] and its supplements.[12] Nevertheless, on this occasion, I shall follow Dodrupchen Rinpoche's explanation to Nyala Rinpoche (Tertön Sogyal).

All phenomena are included within the two categories of object and subject. Just as all knowable phenomena are said to be included within the two truths, all objects are included within the three categories of origin, location, and destination, and all subjects within the three categories of that which arises, that which remains, and that which departs.

First, when examining the origin, you should relate the analysis to a particular basis, by focusing, for example, on a pillar in front of you. When, in the first instant of perceiving the pillar by means of the visual consciousness, you have the thought "It is a pillar," ask yourself, Does this consciousness arise from the pillar or not? At that time, without analyzing the subjective mind, consider only the object pillar and how, while empty in its own essence, it still appears—its aspect of appearance being unobstructed. While appearing, the pillar is primordially empty in essence, with the character of being free from complexity. Without losing its apparent basis, it is empty, and without losing its empty basis, it appears. We must be certain, therefore, that its identity is the union of appearance and emptiness.

Others assert that the pillar is not empty of its own essence but is empty of true existence. Therefore, as true existence does not exist in knowable phenomena, and phenomena themselves, such as vases, are not empty from the perspective of ultimate analysis, appearance and emptiness are not a unity, and there is no relationship of method and outcome, or of the nature of things and things themselves. As true existence does not exist in knowable phenomena, the emptiness that is its absence is also impossible: it is like saying a horse is empty of a cow. Even if such emptiness did exist, there could be no union of appearance and emptiness—they would differ in essence, and it would be like twisting together white and black thread. Of the seven kinds of emptiness, including the trivial, mentioned in the *Laṅkāvatāra Sūtra*,[13] one thing being empty of another—as in the absence of the child of a barren woman, or of a rabbit's horn, or when a pauper is devoid of wealth—is the trivial kind of emptiness. It is not the kind of emptiness that someone desirous of liberation should cultivate or meditate upon.

There are those who claim that while a pillar itself is not empty from the perspective of ultimate analysis, it is empty of true existence. Even if there were an impression of true existence and the like, unless the pillar itself was empty, it would have the character of being truly existent, permanent, stable, and unchanging. Lama Gyade said, "Even if you assert that a pillar is empty of its own essence, you accept that emptiness is freedom from conceptual elaboration. And it is meaningless to suggest that the emptiness resulting from the negation of a thing's apparent aspect is freedom from conceptual elaboration." The followers of this tradition might say to Mipham, If it is necessary for the union of appearance and emptiness to be present all the time, the features of a pale wooden pillar must also be present even during the noble ones' wisdom of meditative equipoise. Even if Mipham did not address such an objection directly, it is refuted by this system's assertions.

When investigating the subject, if we take visual consciousness as an example, the quality of cognizing and being aware of an object is itself an outward sign of the genuine wisdom of clear light. The definition of consciousness is, after all, "that which cognizes and is aware." Consciousness is what makes the unknown known, what cognizes the uncognized, what realizes the unrealized. Of course, this does not mean it literally *illuminates* in the way a lamp does.[14] As an outward sign of great empty basic space, free from conceptual elaboration, consciousness is, in essence, originally empty and free from conceptual elaboration. And as the outward sign of the union of space and wisdom, these two—consciousness and its emptiness—have the character of being inseparably united.

Thus, like the cubs of a white snow lioness, we possess signs of a pure heritage.

Dodrup Rinpoche used to say that this inseparable union of space and wisdom lies at the heart of all phenomena: it is, in a sense, their vital force, or hallmark. And all that can be perceived right now, therefore, is included within this buddha nature or genuine clear light. Nothing whatsoever is excluded. Pointing his finger,[15] he would say, "All this—the peaks and the hollows—is just the same."

Dodrup Rinpoche would also say that the three parts of preparation, main part, and conclusion must be complete. And when they are complete, anyone who meditates on this view of coming, staying, and going for three years will be able to gain liberation during the intermediate state, even if they were to die before ever meditating upon trekchö itself. This is excellent and is not how it is usually understood. Such a practitioner would indeed have gained the certainty that all that appears in the intermediate state is the union of appearance and emptiness. For the duration of meditative equipoise, there would be no clinging, not even to the four extremes, to permanence and nonexistence, or to the self-identity of an individual or phenomena, and so on. This is to have set out on the path; it is also the Great Perfection.

In short, all phenomena without exception, whether they belong to saṃsāra, nirvāṇa, or the path, are the union of absolute space and wisdom, or the union of appearance and emptiness. On the impure, saṃsāric plane, all that appears, without even the slightest exception, is the union of appearance and emptiness. At the time of the ultimate fruition too, appearances that arise out of the space of great, primordial emptiness—the pure realms and buddha forms—appear as the limitless, self-manifesting array of wisdom. And at the stage when yogis are on the path, there is direct realization of the natural state of all phenomena, which is the union of absolute space and wisdom. Then, during the postmeditation phase, perceptions arise as the union of appearance and emptiness, illusory and insubstantial.

Lama Nyala once asked Dodrup Rinpoche whether there was any qualitative distinction between the view of coming, staying, and going in this context and the Middle Way view. Rinpoche replied that there is a difference. "The Middle Way," he said, "corresponds to the sūtras, above which are the three Tantra classes of the Mantra Vehicle, and beyond those, the three inner Tantra classes of mantra. It is among these final three classes that we find the very pinnacle of all nine vehicles, the Great Perfection or Atiyoga. So there is a difference."

Tertön Tsang (Tertön Sogyal) would say, "Aside from this distinction in terms of the basis, there is also a great difference in the features themselves." When he was asked, "Well then, must there be a philosophical standpoint[16] or not?" he replied, "If there were, this would not be breaking down the house of the mind so much as constructing it." When told that Lama Lungtok says there must be a philosophical standpoint, he said, "Oh yes, he does say that." So, while Lama Nyala says there should be no standpoint, Lama Lungtok said there must be. When Lama Tsang (Yukhok Chatralwa) was asked, "How do you believe it is?" he said he too did not think there should be a standpoint.[17]

Then, when asked what are the distinctive features over and above the difference in the basis itself, the lama said that here, when settling with ease in meditative equipoise, based on a lamp-like certainty as to the union of appearance and emptiness, there is no philosophical standpoint whatsoever related to the four extremes. The sign of this is that whatever arises within the basic space of the essence of mind can do so without obstruction—and this is a special feature not found in the Middle Way.

On the path of trekchö, the arising and liberation of thoughts occur simultaneously. So, at that stage, as a sign that the view of coming, staying, and going has pervaded the mind stream, there is self-liberation without the need for any other antidote. And this is another special feature not to be found in the Middle Way.

Although the path of trekchö generally involves the simultaneous arising and liberation of thoughts, this practice (of coming, staying, and going) does not feature the genuine form of liberation upon arising, as that belongs only to the main practice. Still, it does mark the point at which such liberation upon arising begins, and that is why it is considered a trekchö preliminary.

There is a further point here concerning the investigation of coming, staying, and going. As adventitious, delusory appearances are absent at the time of the original ground, they are empty in terms of their origin. Nor is there anywhere that such appearances remain in the interim—they are all just as transient as an unexpected guest. They are like the falling hairs that appear in the sky for someone with an eye disorder, or the sight of a yellow conch to someone with jaundice, or water in its frozen state. As such analogies indicate, appearances are by nature adventitious; they constantly arise afresh and are therefore without any abiding essence. Finally, as such phenomena are absent at the time of the ultimate fruition, they are also empty in terms of their destination.

As Rongzom, Longchenpa, Mipham, and others have asserted, when establishing appearances as divine and the subjective mind as wisdom, conventional valid cognition has two aspects: that based on narrow, limited vision and that based on vision that is pure. If we consider only the first of these, it is impossible, from the perspective of either valid direct perception or valid inference, for pure appearances to derive from impure appearances. Considering the second, however, from the perspective of the wisdom that is present in the meditative equipoise of noble beings, the fading of all dualistic perception means that the dualism of clinging to subject and object is definitively averted. And, even during the postmeditation phase, appearances arise without being taken as real. Then, on the eighth bodhisattva level, during the postmeditation phase, appearance and existence dawn as infinite purity. In the pure perception of the buddhas, the vision, within even a single atom, of inconceivable pure realms, each containing teachers together with their retinues, as numerous as atoms, is the valid cognition of the ultimate vision of how things are. As this is the valid cognition of ultimate vision, we can realize how all the delusory appearances that we currently have as ordinary beings are not truly valid but are in fact false and deceptive.

A sign of pure awareness (rigpa) is that no ordinary thought will arise. Neither potential deviations nor the slightest stains of ordinary mind should be present. All thoughts should arise with the quality of pure awareness. Just as when the sun rises there is no possibility for darkness or gloom to remain, when pure awareness dawns, all thoughts should arise with rigpa's features.

As for maintaining mindfulness and awareness, when you have mindfulness, you have meditation, and when you let mindfulness slip away, meditation also slips away. Being "mindful and aware" here means being continually cognizant, continually present.

Meditative equipoise should be relaxed. Within such a state, any mental expressions that arise will be freed before they have the chance to create habitual impressions—and this is what we call postmeditation. During ordinary daily activity, pure awareness must be more concentrated. As Mipham says:

> Pith instructions are like children's games.
> Meditation is like the king of mountains or the ocean.

In the primordial ground, beyond transition or change, the
  original experience
Is the guru of primordial purity, beyond the mind and free of
  complexity;
To this guru, while experiencing my own undeluded awareness,
  I pray:
Grant your blessings so I may attain enlightenment in this very
  life!

Revealer of pure awareness, which has never known delusion,
Original lord, primordially awakened,
Recalling your kindness, I pray to you:
Grant your blessings so the world and its inhabitants may be
  liberated as dharmakāya!

The dharmakāya guru of awareness and emptiness
Wrote this to fulfill the wishes of the child of awareness.
May the mantra protectress guard over it
And prevent it from falling into samaya breakers' hands!

Samaya. Sealed. Sealed. Sealed.

12

Playing a Flute in
an Empty Valley

Dongak Chökyi Gyatso (1903–1957) was the incarnation of Alak Dongak, who featured in chapter 2. The teacher who made this identification and supervised the young tulku's education was Amdo Geshe Jampal Rolwe Lodrö, whose appeal for sectarian harmony featured in chapter 10. The relationship between Alak Dongak and Amdo Geshe is unclear, partly because so little information is available on Alak Dongak's life. Dongak Chökyi Gyatso's biography is available, however, and therefore we know that he was Amdo Geshe's main disciple, the recipient of instructions on Geluk thought and practice as well as on the Great Perfection.

Dongak Chökyi Gyatso's surviving works contain several texts on Dzogchen, some of which involve comparisons with the Geluk forms of Highest Yoga Tantra. In writing about the Great Perfection, Dongak Chökyi Gyatso followed not only Amdo Geshe but also another of his teachers, Drakkar Tulku Lobzang Palden Tendzin Nyendrak (1866–1928). The latter was an opponent (and later a student) of Mipham. But in addition to his two teachers, Dongak Chökyi Gyatso also emulated his own previous incarnation, Japa Dongak, whose Dzogchen treatise does not survive, as it was burned, so the story goes, after he lost his famous debate with Mipham.

In his treatises, Dongak Chökyi Gyatso does not simply explain Dzogchen on its own terms, as his teachers had done; he seeks instead to reconcile Dzogchen with mainstream Geluk thought. *The Jeweled Mirror Establishing a Single View of the New and Ancient Traditions of Secret Mantra*, for instance, is a prose text in twenty points, which seeks to prove that certain key tenets of Tsongkhapa are compatible with the Nyingma views of Rongzom Chökyi Zangpo and Longchen Rabjam. And *The Offering Clouds of Nectar: A Path of Reasoning Establishing the Single Viewpoint of the Scholars of New and Ancient Traditions* is a verse summary of *The Jeweled Mirror*, written later and covering the same twenty points. In his introduction to *The Jeweled Mirror*, Dongak Chökyi Gyatso states explicitly that his project is nonsectarian. He says he has seen how the traditions of Ancient and New Translations only appear to differ but ultimately share a single point of view. He intends, therefore, to resolve difficult points by means of scripture and reasoning. He is aware that such an undertaking is unlikely to please those who seek only to sow dissension but will persist all the same, "like a herdsman playing a flute in an empty valley." His text focuses on what he calls the "two great traditions" of the Nyingma and "the peerless Riwo Gendenpa." In the current age, he says, with the general degeneration in views and the extreme rarity of any proper assessment based on scripture and reasoning, these two traditions are thought to be contradictory. But his text is a means of dispelling the darkness of such sectarian division and will therefore help others avoid the grievous fault of rejecting the Dharma.

In "Memorandum on Mahāmudrā and Dzogchen Instructions," translated below, Dongak Chökyi Gyatso makes a distinction between "teachings that apply more generally" and "teachings that are intended for individuals." The advanced instructions of Dzogchen (and Mahāmudrā) are suitable only for those of especially high capacity, he explains, and could pose a risk if taught indiscriminately. Even though these advanced instructions are extremely powerful, he says, "this potency is dependent on the level of students' faculties, and it is crucial that the instructions are not misapplied." He claims that Dzogchen's own followers have failed to recognize this: they mistakenly believe that their own teachings can be made available indiscriminately, even to those just setting out on the path. This then allows him to extol the virtues of *lam-*

rim, the graduated path that provides a useful foundation for students of all capacities, without potential risk or danger. This claim that Dzogchen students did not follow a gradual path is disputable. After all, texts such as Patrul Rinpoche's *Words of My Perfect Teacher* set out a path that begins with the ordinary and extraordinary preliminaries (incorporating instructions found in other traditions) and then continues with the levels of the main practice before culminating in Dzogchen, which, as we have seen, has its own preliminary practices too.[1] Yet this is not to say that every teacher of the tradition always adhered to such a gradual presentation. In any case, Dongak Chökyi Gyatso is also critical of Gelukpa teachers who fail to acknowledge the existence of swifter paths, in the belief "that Mahāmudrā and Dzogchen and the like are unacceptable" and that the Kagyü and Nyingma are evil.

As a Gelukpa who accepts the validity of the Dzogchen teachings, Dongak Chökyi Gyatso advocates an intermediate course. He seeks to avoid what we might call Dzogchen (and/or Mahāmudrā) elitism on the one hand and a more exclusivist form of Gelukpa gradualism on the other. Most practitioners must proceed gradually, he says, beginning with what he calls the scriptural approach. But in exceptional cases there are those for whom direct access to the highest doctrines of Dzogchen or Mahāmudrā is appropriate.

Dongak Chökyi Gyatso was not the first Gelukpa to write about Dzogchen, but his comparativism was unusual. And while his texts had only limited impact at the time of their composition, they are currently reaching a wider audience through occasional citations by His Holiness the Dalai Lama.

The personal memorandum that follows concludes with what Dongak Chökyi Gyatso tells us was the final testament of his teacher, Amdo Geshe: "Keep the eyes of your intelligence directed upward, and pay no heed to hollow pronouncements of what is Sarma or what is Nyingma." Although lineage plays an important role in transmission (one to which Dongak Chökyi Gyatso implicitly testifies by recalling his guru's words), adopting and clinging to a position out of loyalty to tradition is ultimately no better or more helpful than any other form of attachment. That the absolute, beyond the ordinary mind, transcends all such distinctions and considerations hardly needs pointing out. But even at a more relative, conventional level, borrowed ideas are useful only to the extent that they can be converted into (or inspire) individual experience and realization. Such is the universal message of the following ostensibly personal memorandum.

Memorandum on Mahāmudrā and Dzogchen Instructions

Dongak Chökyi Gyatso

What follows is a reminder to myself.

The Mahāmudrā and Dzogchen instructions are not invalid. In fact, their validity becomes clear when we make a distinction between (1) teachings that apply more generally[2] and (2) teachings that are intended for individuals.[3]

Regarding the latter, for those of exceptionally high capacity, the ways in which emptiness is introduced, as well as all the various modes of meditation, do not employ the general terminology of the great scriptural traditions of the two pioneering systems of the Mahāyāna. Instead, the teacher points out the way things are, in connection with the Mantra Vehicle, in a state of "ordinary awareness" that does not need to be modified or transformed. Moreover, this inexpressible natural state, free from evaluation, which is the meaning of what is pointed out, is sustained in a natural way. This approach thus unites the entry points to both the common practice of insight and the uncommon practice of taking clear light as the path. Therefore, even though these instructions are extremely powerful, this potency is dependent on the level of students' faculties. And it is crucial that the instructions are not misapplied, as in the example of Devadatta eating medicinal butter.[4]

In the approach that covers the teachings in general, it is of fundamental importance to teach from the beginner's perspective, so that there is no possibility of hindrance or going astray. This would include explanations of how the object of negation is to be identified in the beginning; how it is to be refuted through reasoning;

and how insight is to be sustained through the alternation of analytical and settling meditation on the two types of selflessness, as discovered through the power of reasoning. In this approach, there are separate ways of practicing meditation upon emptiness relating to sūtra and mantra, each making use of methods from their own level, and they are not brought together as one.

These days, however, if you consult followers of Mahāmudrā, Dzogchen, and the like, they will not make even the slightest acknowledgment of instructions that suit people's actual capacity, such as the way to progress in tranquillity and insight as taught in the scriptural approach of the great pioneers. Instead, they will suggest that everyone follow the path of Mahāmudrā or Dzogchen right from the beginning, and declare that anything else is not even Dharma. This only goes to show that the general approach to the teachings has become as inaccessible and remote as flesh-eating spirits!

Furthermore, among the learned followers of the great scriptural approach, those with the greatest knowledge of the Dharma deny any possibility of a distinction between general and particular. Instead, they refute it. Those of lesser learning, on the other hand, simply believe that Mahāmudrā and Dzogchen and the like are unacceptable, and they regard schools such as the Kagyü and Nyingma as evil. Thus, with the existence of an approach tailored to individuals as unapparent as invisible flesh-eating spirits, serious dissensions have emerged. Due to degenerate views, then, attitudes are extremely immature and people lack the intellectual strength required to bear the weight of the Mahāyāna.

The teachings tailored to individuals are not only extremely effective, but they can also be the basis for great confusion. There are many who have been led astray, mistaking trinkets for jewels, while thinking they have chanced upon some treasure bequeathed by the great masters of the past.

There are no obstacles at all to the approach of investigating and concluding with immaculate reasoning in the scriptural tradition of the scholars of India. Tracing back the lineage of this approach, you will find Maitreya and Mañjuśrī and, ultimately, the perfect Buddha himself. Whatever you think of this teaching, which we refer to as the Dharma, it is a gradual path to enlightenment combining all that is to be trained in by the three types of individual in a form that can be practiced in a single session, on a single seat. I cannot bear the thought that I might die without first planting the habitual seeds for such a teaching. Yet, as the saying goes, "The Lord of Death does not wait for all our tasks to be completed." So, I must establish such habitual tendencies today. And, from now on, through daily reaffirmation, I shall strengthen this impression on my mind.

From the very depths of my heart, I take refuge in the Kagyü, Nyingma, and other schools. Yet I shall not practice, even in my dreams, any form of Sakya, Kagyü, or Nyingma in which the scriptural tradition of the great pioneers is disregarded or abandoned.

Not only in this life but in all my lives to come, I aspire to serve the teachings of the second Buddha, Tsongkhapa. Yet, even at the cost of my life, I shall never practice any form of Geluk that regards its own view as supreme and treats all types of individual as if they were the same, blanketing them all under a single approach to the Dharma or means of training.

In short, I shall always follow my supreme guide, the Lord of Dharma, who gained full realization and mastery of all the teachings and, in the account of his liberation, offered the following advice as his final testament: "Keep the eyes of your intelligence directed upward, and pay no heed to hollow pronouncements of what is Sarma or what is Nyingma."

ACKNOWLEDGMENTS

The translator wishes to express his deepest gratitude to Alak Zenkar Rinpoche, who generously contributed a foreword, patiently answered many questions, elaborated upon the history of people and places, and generally lived up to his reputation as a walking, talking encyclopedia of all things Tibetan Buddhist. Tulku Thondup Rinpoche too made this book possible, not only through his wonderful writings on the masters and topics featured in these pages, but also by kindly agreeing to be interviewed, thereby contributing material for the introductory essays, and by clarifying several difficult points in the translation. Ringu Tulku Rinpoche also provided invaluable assistance, as did the late Khenpo Dorje. In this project and more generally, Sogyal Rinpoche and Patrick Gaffney, through their patient guidance and encouragement, have shown time and again what it really means to translate the Dharma and to communicate it with due care and attention. (Needless to say, however, any errors or inadequacies in the present volume remain the translator's sole responsibility.) Fastidious readers of early drafts included Douglas Duckworth, Ani Ngawang Tsöndrü, Philip Philippou, and Lucie Cohen, all of whom made valuable suggestions. Thanks are also due to Janine Schulz, Nikko Odiseos, Sean Price, Gyurmé Avertin, Casey Kemp, Tracy Davis, and all the team at Shambhala Publications for their kindness and much needed expertise.

Notes

Introduction

1. Throughout this book, "ordinary mind" is used to translate the Tibetan term *sems*, which is the ordinary discursive mind that in Dzogchen is often contrasted with *rigpa*, the pure awareness that transcends the ordinary mind. The Mahāmudrā (and occasionally Dzogchen) term *tha mal gyi shes pa*, which some translate as "ordinary mind," is here translated—on the few occasions where it occurs—as "ordinary awareness," or "ordinary consciousness."

2. Orgyen Tendzin Norbu is not always listed among Jigme Tenpe Nyima's teachers, but the latter refers to him as "our noble teacher" in his commentary on his final words. See page 62.

1. A Yogi's Guide to the Dharma

1. For a brief biography based on the most up-to-date sources, see Pearcey, "Pema Vajra," at www.treasuryoflives.org, 2012.

2. The figure of six volumes is given in the biography by Wangchen Dargye ("mKhan chen padma badzra rim byon gyi rnam thar") in Padma Badzra, *rDzogs chen mkhan chen padma badzra'i gsung thor bu* (Chengdu: Si khron mi rigs dpe skrun khang, 2001), 8–13, which is translated and published on lotsawahouse.org. A single-volume block print of his writings was published in the 1990s; this then became the source for a short paperback edition of miscellaneous works in 2001. A two-volume paperback edition of his collected writings was published in 2011.

3. Taken from the famous aspiration prayer called *Samantabhadra's Aspiration to Good Actions* (*bZang spyod smon lam*).

4. *oṃ ye dharmā hetu prabhāvā hetuṃ teṣāṃ tathāgato hyavadat teṣāṃ ca yo nirodha evaṃ vādī mahāśramaṇaḥ svāhā.*

2. The Consolation of Solitude

1. In Golok he is known chiefly with the honorific as Alak Dongak, but elsewhere in Kham he is often referred to as Japa Dongak. Unfortunately,

there seems to be no consensus on how to spell Japa: some sources have 'Gya['] pa, others 'Ja' pa or even 'Bya ba, and there are some texts that alternate between them.

2. Kun bzang dpal ldan, *Gangs ri'i khrod kyi smra ba'i seng ge gcig pu 'jam mgon mi pham rgya mtsho'i rnam thar snying po bsdus pa*, 22.

3. Mi-pam-gya-tso, *Fundamental Mind: The Nyingma View of the Great Completeness*, 24–25.

4. Personal communication, October 2014.

5. Janet Gyatso used this expression and made this point during her talk (attended by the author) as part of a memorial panel in honor of the late E. Gene Smith held at Columbia University on February 12, 2011.

6. Ārya Asaṅga's commentary on the *Mahāyānasūtrālaṃkāra* explains the seven kinds of attachment (*chags bdun*) in connection with the pāramitā of generosity as (1) attachment to possessions, (2) postponing the practice, (3) being satisfied with just a little practice, (4) expectation of something in return, (5) karmic results, (6) adverse circumstances, and (7) distractions.

3. THE RIMÉ OF THE ANCIENTS' MONK-SCHOLAR

1. *lam dus*, i.e., a brief Hevajra sādhana.

2. In Tibetan, Mahāmudrā (Great Seal) is often abbreviated from its full form, *phyag rgya chen po*, to *phyag chen*, which literally means simply "great hand."

3. (1) All that is conditioned is impermanent, (2) all that is tainted is suffering, (3) all phenomena are empty and devoid of self, and (4) nirvāṇa is peace.

4. I.e., the meaning rather than the words, the actual tantra (or continua) of ground, path, and fruition, rather than the written tantras. (Alak Zenkar Rinpoche)

5. I.e., the Gelukpas.

4. ANALYSIS AND WHAT LIES BEYOND

1. "The Wheel of Analytical Meditation" is available in translation on lotsawahouse.org and in Dilgo Khyentse, *The Collected Works of Dilgo Khyentse*, Vol. 2 (Boston: Shambhala Publications, 2010), 125–31.

2. Some editions of the Tibetan have *khong snyom*, but Alak Zenkar Rinpoche believes this is an error for *khod snyom*.

3. The term "realized one" in the title can be understood either in a strictly literal sense to mean a highly realized individual or in its more colloquial sense of yogi or meditator. In his commentary on the title, Khangsar Tenpe Wangchuk explains that the expression here refers to those whose study may be weak but who maintain the profound instructions as the core of their practice.

4. This is a reference to five successive experiences that occur during the development of meditation in general and śamatha in particular. They are termed movement (compared to a cascade of water down a rock face), attainment (compared to a torrent in a deep ravine), familiarization (a meandering river), stability (an ocean free of waves), and consummation (a mountain, or lamp that is unmoved by the wind).

5. Here Mipham plays on the literal meaning of the Tibetan term for Buddha or enlightenment (*sangs rgyas*), which consists of two syllables meaning "cleared away or purified" (*sangs*) and "unfolded or expanded" (*rgyas*).

5. A Midlife Crisis (of Allegiance)

1. There is significance to these positions: *gung* means noon or midnight, while *thang* refers to a plain.

2. bSod nams nyi ma, *Grub rje sku phreng rim par byon pa'i rnam par thar pa 'dod 'byung nor bu'i phreng ba*,81–82.

3. Ibid.,82–83.

4. According to Alak Zenkar Rinpoche, read *byes* as *byis*.

5. The translation of this line is tentative.

6. These two lines appear in Thondup, *Masters of Meditation and Miracles*, 241.

7. I.e., the Longde (*klong sde*).

8. *Sita tshattraṃ*, presumably a Tibetan transcription of the Sanskrit *Sitachattra*, meaning "white parasol," an alternative name for the deity Sitātapatrā.

6. The Final Roar of a Scholar-Lion

1. bsTan 'dzin lung rtogs nyi ma, *sNga 'gyur rdzogs chen chos 'byung chen mo*, 594–95.

2. It is illustrative to compare Orgyen Tendzin Norbu's final words with the famous four-line testament of Minling Terchen Gyurme Dorje (1646–1714), which refers exclusively to Higher Tantra: "May appearance, sound,

and awareness in the state of deity, mantra, and dharmakāya / Merge boundlessly as the display of kāyas and wisdoms / In the profound and secret practice of the great yoga, / And may they be of one taste, indivisible within the sphere of the enlightened mind." (*snang grags rig gsum lha sngags chos sku'i ngang/ sku dang ye shes rol par 'byams klas pas/ zab gsang rnal 'byor chen po'i nyams len la/ dbyer med thugs kyi thig ler ro gcig shog/*)

7. A Little Learning is a Dangerous Thing

1. It has no title in the original Tibetan.

2. Longchen Rabjam, it should be noted, studied in his youth at Sangpu Neutok, a Kadampa monastery famed for its scholarly tradition. His own writings also warn of the limitations of scholasticism, as when in *A Mirror Revealing the Crucial Points: Advice on the Ultimate Meaning,* he states, "If realization does not dawn from within, dry explanations and theoretical understanding will not bring the fruit of awakening." During his lifetime, however, the Nyingma did not have a well-developed scholastic tradition of its own.

3. *shes gnyen yon tan gyi bdud.* The term occurs in Patrul Rinpoche's *Total Victory over the Māras: An Instruction on How to Diagnose the Causes of Demonic Influence and Overcome Them (bDud kyi rgyu brtags te spong tshul gyi man ngag bdud las rnam rgyal).* My translation of the term is based on Ringu Tulku Rinpoche's oral explanation.

8. Remembrance of Awareness Present

1. Amdo Geshe's comments are recorded in *A skong mkhan chen blo bzang rdo rje'i gsung 'bum,* vol. 4, 38. Dongak Chökyi Gyatso's panegyric, called *gZungs kyi rnam bshad la bstod pa,* is found in *sNyan dgon sprul sku' gsung rab pa'i gsung 'bum,* vol. 3, 57–58.

2. It is likely that the devoted Gyurme Dorje of the title is the same individual whom Jigme Tenpe Nyima refers to in similar terms in another text of more general advice, specifying additionally that he is "from the land of Samsa to the east" (*shar phyogs bsam sa'i yul gyi*). See *rDo grub chen 'jigs med bstan pa'i nyi ma'i gsung 'bum,* vol. 1, 433–36.

3. Lhatsün Namkha Jigme (1597–1693).

4. *Dur khrod phung po 'bar ba'i rgyud.* A tantra from the *Collection of Nyingma Tantras (rNying ma rgyud 'bum).*

5. A very similar statement is found in the writings of Jigme Lingpa, but I

have not located this quotation within the works of Longchen Rabjam. It is possible, therefore, that "Omniscient One" here refers to Jigme Lingpa.

6. *Khregs chod kyi yang yig nam mkha' klong yangs*, a text by Longchen Rabjam, included in the collection known as *Four Sections of the Heart Essence* (*sNying thig ya bzhi*).

9. A Portrait of the Master as a Young Tulku

1. In *The Sun, Moon, Planets, and Stars*, Longchen Rabjam explains the two powers as follows: "'Power over creation' refers to the instantaneous display of emanations to guide beings in appropriate ways. It is the capacity to liberate three thousand beings in an instant by directing one's pure awareness at them. 'Power over animation' is the capacity to move material objects and cause them to speak by directing pure awareness toward them. One thereby guides beings by producing the sound of the Dharma from lotuses, wish-granting trees, and so on, and through miracles and emanating light." (*Thod rgal gyi rgyab yig nyi zla gza' skar. Kun mkhyen klong chen rab 'byams kyi gsung 'bum*, vol. 9, 275).

2. The most important commentary on *The Essence of the Eight Branches*, written by Candranandana.

3. I have been unable to locate this section of *Dispelling the Darkness of the Ten Directions*.

4. The seven riches of the absolute (*don dam dkor bdun*) are enlightened body, speech, mind, qualities, and activity, plus the dharmadhātu and primordial wisdom.

5. In his *Key to the Precious Treasury* commentary on the *Guhyagarbha Tantra*, Jigme Tenpe Nyima explains, "The two common forms are that all phenomena are equal in being unborn on an absolute level and illusory on a relative level."

6. Jigme Lingpa's *Treasury of Precious Qualities* to which Jigme Lingpa himself wrote two autocommentaries: *Chariot of the Two Truths* and *Chariot of Omniscience*.

10. Please Debate the Messenger

1. My translation of his text in praise of Longchen Rabjam can be found on lotsawahouse.org.

2. *Kārikas* here refers to the *Verses for Novices* (*Śrāmaṇerakārikā*).

3. Tsongkhapa.

4. Śarabha, the king of lions in Hindu mythology.
5. The three collections are Vinaya, Sūtra, and Abhidharma.
6. The four classes of Tantra are Action (*Kriyā*), Performance (*Caryā*), Yoga, and Highest (or Unsurpassed) Yoga.
7. The three visions (*snang gsum*) or three levels of spiritual perception are the impure vision of ordinary beings, the partially purified vision of those on the path, and the pure vision of fully enlightened buddhas.
8. The three continua (*rgyud gsum*) are the causal continuum of the ground-of-all, the method continuum of the body, and the resultant continuum of the ultimate fruition.
9. This is seemingly a reference to the views of Taktsang Lotsāwa Sherab Rinchen, who denies the existence of any form of valid cognition in Prāsaṅgika-Madhyamaka in his major work, *Understanding All Tenets* (*Grub mtha' kun shes*). There he argues that since everything is deceptive, there can be no valid cognition (*pramāṇa*) which is generally defined as undeceptive. The non-Buddhist Cārvāka school accepts a single form of valid cognition, that of direct perception. (Many thanks to Douglas Duckworth for clarifying the significance of this verse.)
10. The Five Patriarchs or founding figures of the Sakya tradition were Sachen Kunga Nyingpo (1092–1158), together with his two sons, Sönam Tsemo (1142–1182) and Drakpa Gyaltsen (1147–1216), and his grandson, Sakya Paṇḍita (1182–1251), as well as the latter's nephew, Chögyal Pakpa Lodrö Gyaltsen (1235–1280).
11. The traditions of Nāgārjuna and Asaṅga, respectively.
12. The indivisibility of samsāra and nirvāna ('*khor 'das dbyer med*) is a central tenet of the Sakya tradition.
13. According to the Sakya scholar Drakpa Gyaltsen, the three major commentaries of Candrakīrti are his explanations of Āryadeva's *Four Hundred Verses* (*Catuḥśataka*) and Nāgārjuna's *Reason Sixty* (*Yuktiṣaṣṭikā*), as well as his own *Prasannapadā*, which is a commentary on Nāgārjuna's famous *Madhyamakakārikā*.
14. The six limits are provisional meaning, definitive meaning, indirect, not indirect, literally true, and not literally true. The four modes are literal, general, hidden, and ultimate.
15. This verse is not found in the *Viśeṣa-stotra*, so its origin is unclear.

11. DEMOLITION, DZOGCHEN STYLE

1. From *The Beacon of Certainty* (*Nges shes sgron me*).
2. From *Vajra Mortar* (*rDo rje'i gtun khung*).

3. From *Instructions on Trekchö*.

4. The text is seemingly a set of notes taken by an anonymous student. The expression "he said/would say" (*gsungs*), referring to Yukhok Chatralwa, appears throughout the Tibetan text but has not been reproduced in the translation.

5. It is the third of the text's seven topics.

6. bSod nams nyi ma, *Grub rje sku phreng rim par byon pa'i rnam par thar pa 'dod 'byung nor bu'i phreng ba*, 110.

7. Following Alak Zenkar Rinpoche, I am reading *a gtad* as *ar gtad* here.

8. *Uttaratantra*, verse 14cd.

9. Literally, "six and a fraction" (*nyi tshe zhig dang bdun*), meaning six major plus some minor traditions. The figure is unusual, and I have not been able to identify exactly which schools are meant, although the four major schools of Nyingma, Sakya, Kagyü, and Geluk are almost certainly included, possibly with the addition of the Jonang and Shije.

10. In most versions of these preliminaries, this question of whether body, speech or mind is most important belongs to the first investigation, as Yukhok Chatralwa makes clear in his opening remarks. It might therefore be best to understand the discussion at this point in the text as something akin to a footnote.

11. *Khregs chod ye babs sor bzhag*, a manual written by Longchen Rabjam.

12. This would seem to be a reference to *Vast Expanse of Space* (*Nam mkha' klong yangs*), a supplement on trekchö, and *Great Expanse of Space* (*Nam mkha' klong chen*), a supplement on both trekchö and tögal. All these texts, including *Settling into Natural Rest Through Trekchö*, are from the Lama Yangtik collection, which is in turn part of the *Four-Part Heart Essence* (*sNying thig ya bzhi*).

13. The seven forms of emptiness mentioned in the *Laṅkāvatāra Sūtra* are: (1) emptiness of characteristics (*mtshan nyid stong pa nyid*); (2) emptiness of the nature of entities (*dngos po'i rang bzhin stong pa nyid*); (3) emptiness of becoming (*srid pa'i stong pa nyid*); (4) emptiness of non-becoming (*mi srid pa stong pa nyid*); (5) inexpressible emptiness (*brjod du med pa'i stong pa nyid*); (6) emptiness of the ultimate great wisdom of the noble ones (*don dam pa 'phags pa'i ye shes chen po stong pa nyid*); and (7) emptiness of one thing in another (*gcig gis gcig stong pa nyid*).

14. The final phrase (*mar me lta bu*) is added as an editor's note in the Tibetan.

15. Once again, this expression appears as a note in the original text.

16. *'dzin stangs*, sometimes translated as "modal apprehension," is the deliberate focusing upon, or maintaining of, a (philosophical) notion in meditation.

17. The fact that Yukhok Chatralwa is here cited in his own text underscores the point that this was compiled by an anonymous editor.

12. PLAYING A FLUTE IN AN EMPTY VALLEY

1. The Nyingma/Dzogchen tradition also gained its own answer to *lamrim* with the revelation of the *Lamrim Yeshe Nyingpo* by Chokgyur Dechen Lingpa and Jamyang Khyentse Wangpo in the nineteenth century.

2. *bstan pa spyi btsan.*

3. *gang zag sgos btsan.*

4. On one occasion, when the Buddha and his monks fell sick in Śrāvasti, he was advised by the doctor, Kumārā Jīvaka, to take twelve measures of powerful medicinal butter, while all the other monks were instructed to take no more than a single measure. Devadatta, claiming that he was of the same family as the Buddha, insisted on taking two measures, but nearly died as a result and was saved only through the Buddha's miraculous intervention.

Texts Translated

Chapter 1

Padma badzra. "'Khor lo gsum dang rig 'dzin sngags kyi sde snod bcas pa'i don bsdus." In *mKhan chen padma badzra'i gsung 'bum*. 2 vols. Lhasa: Bod ljongs bod yig dpe rnying dpe skrun khang, 2011. Vol. 1, 363–72.

Chapter 2

O rgyan 'jigs med chos kyi dbang po. "Phyi nang gi dben pa ya ma bral bar bsten tshul sogs 'ja' ba mdo sngags la gdams pa." In *O rgyan 'jigs med chos kyi dbang po'i gsung 'bum*. Chengdu: Si khron mi rigs dpe skrun khang, 2009. Vol. 8, 237–43.

Chapter 3

Mi pham. "Grogs dang gtam gleng ba'i rkyen las mtshar gtam du byas pa." In *Mi pham gsung 'bum*. 32 vols. Chengdu: Gangs can rig gzhung dpe rnying myur skyobs lhan tshogs, 2007. Vol. 7, 229–33.

———. "Bod yul chos lugs rnam pa bzhi." In ibid. Vol. 32, 410.

Chapter 4

Mi pham. "dBu ma'i lta khrid zab mo." In *Mi pham gsung 'bum*. 32 vols. Chengdu: Gangs can rig gzhung dpe rnying myur skyobs lhan tshogs, 2007. Vol. 32, 321–23.

———. "Sems kyi ngo bo." In ibid. Vol. 32, 368–70.

———. "Rig ngo skyong thabs ye shes snying po." In ibid. Vol. 32, 357–60.

———. "Sems kyi rang bzhin." In ibid. Vol. 32, 398–99.

———. "rTogs ldan rgan mo rnams kyi lugs sems ngo mdzub tshugs kyi gdams pa mun sel sgron me." In ibid. Vol. 32, 363–68.

CHAPTER 5

Mi pham. "Kun mkhyen mi pham rin po ches rdo grub sprul sku 'jigs med bstan pa'i nyi mar zhal gdams bslab bya gnang ba." In *Mi pham gsung 'bum.* 27 vols. Paro: Lama Ngodrup and Sherab Drimey, 1984–1993. Vol. 27, 281–84.

CHAPTER 6

'Jigs med bstan pa'i nyi ma. "Dad brtson blo ldan 'das shul grags ldan ngor gdams pa." In *rDo grub chen 'jigs med bstan pa'i nyi ma'i gsung 'bum.* 7 vols. Chengdu: Si khron mi rigs dpe skrun khang, 2003. Vol. 2, 21–25.

CHAPTER 7

'Jigs med bstan pa'i nyi ma. (Untitled.) In *rDo grub chen 'jigs med bstan pa'i nyi ma'i gsung 'bum.* 7 vols. Chengdu: Si khron mi rigs dpe skrun khang, 2003. Vol. 1, 351–54.

CHAPTER 8

'Jigs med bstan pa'i nyi ma. "Dad ldan 'gyur med rdo rje'i ngor gdams pa." In *rDo grub chen 'jigs med bstan pa'i nyi ma'i gsung 'bum.* 7 vols. Chengdu: Si khron mi rigs dpe skrun khang, 2003. Vol. 2, 41–53.

CHAPTER 9

'Jigs med bstan pa'i nyi ma. "rDzogs chen dris lan." In *rDo grub chen 'jigs med bstan pa'i nyi ma'i gsung 'bum.* 7 vols. Chengdu: Si khron mi rigs dpe skrun khang, 2003. Vol. 2, 117–35.

CHAPTER 10

'Jam dpal rol ba'i blo gros. "Lugs gnyis kyi mdun sa chen po sde dge lhun grub steng nas phyogs kyi mkhas pa rnams la spring ba rtsod pa'i skabs rnam par dbye ba'i yi ge yang dag rigs pa'i pho nya." In *A mdo dge bshes 'jam dpal rol ba'i blo gros kyi gsung 'bum.* 2 vols. Chengdu: Si khron mi rigs dpe skrun khang, 2004. Vol. 1, 119–26.

CHAPTER 11

Chos dbyings rang grol. "rDzogs pa chen po'i lam nyams su len tshul." In *Chos dbyings rang grol gsung 'bum*. Chengdu: Si khron mi rigs dpe skrun khang, 2007. Vol. 2, 403–14.

CHAPTER 12

mDo sngags chos kyi rgya mtsho. "Phyag rdzogs gdams pa'i skor gyi brjed tho." In *sNyan dgon sprul sku'i gsung rab pa'i gsung 'bum*. 3 vols. Chengdu: Si khron mi rigs dpe skrun khang, 2006. Vol. 2, 268–71.

Bibliography

Works in Tibetan

Blo bzang rdo rje. *A skong mkhan chen blo bzang rdo rje'i gsung 'bum.* 5 vols. Chengdu: Si khron mi rigs dpe skrun khang, 2003.

bDe legs rab rgyas. "rTsam pa po'i ngo sprod mdor bsdus." In *rDo grub chen 'jigs med bstan pa'i nyi ma'i gsung 'bum.* 7 vols. Chengdu: Si khron mi rigs dpe skrun khang, 2003. Vol. 1, 11–16.

Klong chen rab 'byams. *Kun mkhyen klong chen rab 'byams kyi gsung 'bum.* 26 vols. Beijing: Krung go'i bod rig pa dpe skrun khang, 2009.

Kun bzang dpal ldan. "Gangs ri'i khrod kyi smra ba'i seng ge gcig pu 'jam mgon mi pham rgya mtsho'i rnam thar snying po bsdus pa." In Mi pham, *mKhas pa'i tshul la 'jug pa'i sgo.* Xining: mTsho sngon mi rigs dpe skrun khang, 1988, 1–43

Ngag dbang dpal bzang. *mKhan po ngag chung gi rnam thar.* Chengdu: Si khron mi rigs dpe skrun khang, 2000.

bSod nams nyi ma. *Grub rje sku phreng rim par byon pa'i rnam par thar pa 'dod 'byung nor bu'i phreng ba.* Gangtok: Pema Thinley, 2002.

bsTan 'dzin lung rtogs nyi ma. *sNga 'gyur rdzogs chen chos 'byung chen mo.* Beijing: Krong go'i bod rigs dpe skrun khang, 2004.

Works in English

Dalai Lama, the Fourteenth. *Dzogchen: The Heart Essence of the Great Perfection.* Translated by Geshe Thupten Jinpa and Richard Barron. Ithaca, NY: Snow Lion Publications, 2000.

———. *Mind in Comfort and Ease: The Vision of Enlightenment in the Great Perfection.* Translated by Matthieu Ricard, Richard Barron, and Adam Pearcey. Boston: Wisdom Publications, 2007.

Dilgo Khyentse et al. *The Life and Times of Jamyang Khyentse Chökyi Lodrö: The Great Biography by Dilgo Khyentse Rinpoche and Other Stories.* Boulder: Shambhala Publications, 2017.

Dreyfus, Georges. *The Sound of Two Hands Clapping: The Education of a Tibetan Buddhist Monk*. Berkeley: University of California Press, 2003.

Duckworth, Douglas. *Jamgön Mipam: His Life and Teachings*. Boston: Shambhala Publications, 2011.

Dudjom Rinpoche. *The Nyingma School of Tibetan Buddhism: Its Fundamentals and History*. Translated and edited by Gyurme Dorje and Matthew Kapstein. Boston: Wisdom Publications, 1991.

Germano, David. "Architecture and Absence in the Secret Tantric History of the Great Perfection (*rdzogs chen*)." *Journal of the International Association of Buddhist Studies* 17, no. 2. (1994): 203–335.

Khenpo Ngawang Pelzang. *A Guide to the Words of My Perfect Teacher*. Translated by Padmakara Translation Group. Boston: Shambhala Publications, 2004.

Klein, Anne Carolyn. "Assorted Topics of the Great Completeness by Dodrupchen III." In *Tantra in Practice*. Edited by David Gordon White, 557–72. Princeton, NJ: Princeton University Press, 2000.

Mi-pam-gya-tso. *Fundamental Mind: The Nyingma View of the Great Completeness*. Translated and edited by Jeffrey Hopkins. Ithaca, NY: Snow Lion Publications, 2006.

Nyoshul Khenpo. *A Marvelous Garland of Rare Gems: Biographies of Masters of Awareness in the Dzogchen Lineage*. Translated by Richard Barron. Junction City, CA: Padma Publications, 2005.

Patrul Rinpoche. *The Words of My Perfect Teacher: A Complete Translation of a Classic Introduction to Tibetan Buddhism*. Translated by Padmakara Translation Group. Boston: Shambhala Publications, 1998.

Pearcey, Adam. "A Greater Perfection: Scholasticism, Comparativism, and Issues of Sectarian Identity in Early 20th Century Writings on rDzogs chen." PhD diss., SOAS, University of London, 2018.

———. "Amdo Geshe Jampel Rolpai Lodro." Treasury of Lives (hereafter TOL) (www.treasuryoflives.org). 2012.

———. "Dongak Chokyi Gyatso." TOL. 2013.

———. "Japa Dongak Gyatso." TOL. 2014.

———. "Orgyen Tendzin Norbu." TOL. 2015.

———. "Pema Vajra." TOL. 2012.

Pettit, John Whitney. *Mipham's Beacon of Certainty: Illuminating the View of Dzogchen, the Great Perfection*. Boston: Wisdom Publications, 1999.

Phuntsho, Karma. *Mipham's Dialectics and the Debates on Emptiness*. Abingdon: Routledge, 2005.

Ringu Tulku. *The Ri-me Philosophy of Jamgön Kongtrul the Great*. Boston: Shambhala Publications, 2006.

Smith, E. Gene. *Among Tibetan Texts: History and Literature of the Himalayan Plateau*. Boston: Wisdom Publications, 2001.

Tulku Thondup. *Masters of Meditation and Miracles: The Longchen Nyingthig Lineage of Tibetan Buddhism*. Boston: Shambhala Publications, 1996.

INDEX